THAT WOMAN COULD BE YOU

THAT WOMAN COULD BE YOU

VI KHI NAO + JESSICA ALEXANDER

BLAZEVOX[BOOKS]
Buffalo, New York

publisher of weird little books

BlazeVOX [books]

blazevox.org

21 20 19 18 17 16 15 14 13 12 01 02 03 04 05 06 07 08 09 10 11

BlazeVOX

ACKNOWLEDGMENTS

We would like the following presses and editors: Thank you Ali Raz, Erik Fuhrer, and Kimberly Androlowicz at *Hush,* Jason Teal at *Heavy Feather Review* , Crow Jonah Norlander at *X-ray,* D.C. Wojciech at *Anvil Tongue Books,* Paul Cunningham at *Action Blog,* Susan Lewis at *Posit,* Steve Barbaro at *New Sinews,* Bükem Reitmayer at *Cosmonauts Avenue,* and Jessica Berger, James Tadd Adcox, & Helenmary Sheridan at *Always Crashing.*

CONTENTS

THAT WOMAN
COULD BE YOU

SATAN WAS AN OPTIMIST

On the ride home, the air alert and pleasantly chill, you read a Milton study guide, you'd found in a pile outside. Autumn is something I haven't experienced in years & Satan was egalitarian & God, being hysterical, banished him to Hell. Milton made Satan so highly appealing, he believed God could be defeated. Meanwhile, Eve, a lesbian, asked to work at a distance from Adam. We ate leftovers and chocolate and watched an entirely awful season of *Clickbait*, on fast forward, a show with such sharp twists, & characters that slip off the slick back seats of a narrative taxi into a boredom so monochrome blue & who had room to act beside you?

For a week, our syncopated bleeding halted lovemaking. We resumed - in the middle of the afternoon, sandwiched between a Zoom interview and a mid-day walk to the grocery for chocolate and salt. Your hair, after you released it from a claw clip, was wet like a hand towel on my clavicle and neck. You tasted like a raw evening meal - like an apple scented oyster on a half-shell. Our bodies were in rhythm (like a DVD player and its TV) and the air was full of a docile ambient-like monotone, the kind mixed between the mechanical noise of the dishwasher and the humming of the refrigerator. Even when the dishwasher beeped twice to remind us of its cycle's completion, we were too tired to get to it and turn its alarm back off. I tried to steal your black sweatpants, which I love. But, you warned me it wasn't possible. I did look for them, I searched our closet and our garment drawers. You exited the shower with a colossal cigar dangling off your lower lip - I mean sweatpants hanging from your hips - which you lit with a lighter the size of a spatula and laughed like old De Niro in a recent role, which ='s domestic comedy + De Niro's caricature of De Niro - all this to say, his laughter,

like yours, is still ebullient
& hellborn.

THAT WOMAN COULD BE YOU

The blue night is not sad, sightless, or cramped over an instrument but the sky is viscous as oil paint and the silos glow like grey smiles. You helped stretch my legs, and because my heels had cracked, you rubbed lotion into my feet. We took photographs. In bed, you smiled and said, "Vi, you are a strange woman," and I said, "What do you mean?"

Our periods, in unison and syncopated, transformed us into brittle leaves. Even when we walked in circles around Zeppelin Station, even after you ordered red wine which has plenty of iron, even when I showed you the Great Divide, the bar which took my small body in when the sky roared with immense striated thunder and lightning, even when we walked underneath a Denver scaffold holding hands, even when you ordered a big burger with fried meat layered in white cheese and an herb that made me think of sorrel, even when my rice arrived with my fried chicken looking like one breast of a woman, I thought how easily a woman could get raped running near or along a railroad track using her phone as a makeshift flashlight. That woman could be you, you thought.

And I thought that woman could be me. We slept unfondly early. At 9 pm. My eyes kept seeing the words: I See You over and over again. And later, you understood it was a horror film I would never watch nor swallow. Your period, you reasoned, has been waiting for me. And in waiting, it has oxidized into a chocolate cake neither one of us can eat. Before bed, I stacked two Maxipads on top of one another. We couldn't find my colossal pads the size of two surfboards which prevent me from turning our bed into a biblical river, the one where water transforms to blood.

My hip kissed yours and our lips met frequently so that my body, lathered with love, could fall into a dead cave called sleep. Before bed, we took the elevator to the rooftop. A couple grilled beef, something meaty. And there was a helper, a woman dressed in blue. You'd met her in the laundry room. She complained that no one takes their clothes from the dryers. She must have forgotten you. But you remembered her and the asymmetry of the reunion embarrassed you. The couple, you noticed, starred into their respective phones. You took pictures of me on the roof with Denver being the post-cerulean sky it wants to be.

From the rooftop, we could see the volleyball team playing noisily in Cross Fit's sandy backyard. We could see the train station that takes me to Union Square the mornings of my teaching. And we could see a couple, an adult boy driving his rented scooter, so popular in this city, while his girlfriend wrapped her arms around his slim form. You wanted us to have that experience. That romantic, suburban romance. Maybe this weekend, I say. And, then your breath took me to another floor of your desire where you washed your hands and held me in your basil or was it lilac scented arms.

In the morning, at 5:30, to be precise, I brought a pyramid to work with me. The pyramid was made of banana leaves, sweet rice, pork fat, and mung beans. I left the peanut rice for you, though I do not believe you eat meals with any regularity. You want cool air to lick the sweat from your body. In your phone, there are three new additions to your favorite photographs of me. I am lying on the mattress with my head tilted to the side. In one, I smile slightly up at you through my haze of pain. My teeth, which you love so much, are showing, though they look as if they might slice into my lower lip. Under the fog of acceptance, are the early stages of a distracted grimace; what you call my strangeness.

On the nightstand, sits the slick orange patterned packaging of a maxi-pad, which wrapped itself around my head. *Someone thought of this.* I said. This intricate design because a woman wants a meticulous arrangement of orange and blue diamonds on nights when she's liable to bleed profusely onto white bed sheets. Meanwhile, you sit at a white table, amidst modern and minimal decorations. Egg shell shapes, is what you think. Space Odyssey, you think. You think of me. A warm body. How far we've had to come just to turn forty. Some nights you whisper, don't die.

Last night, your brother, Jim, zoomed into your dream with golden hair and glowing skin. His boyfriend was there. They laughed. They said, his death had been a ruse to get you to call back. April fools! You woke & whispered: I want to live a long time with you. But I still don't understand what makes me strange. I've heard it all my life. From family, friends, and CD Wright, who'd say Vi is beyond unique.

To me, I am ordinary, even boring. I sleep a lot. I don't smoke or do drugs. I have my period. You say you need time to explain. Take a room, you say. Someone is giving a lecture. The other people in the room resist or accept the premise. Meanwhile a sharp pain takes you away only a siren distracts you from dying. So, you don't hear the lecture, but a suicidal song in the angle of the speaker's arm. In any case, you're listening, intently, to a different argument, entirely.

After leaving your exquisite, soft perfervid body, I faced the untouched light of Denver morning with my fading sight. Even without glasses, I could tell that the city has a silhouette and that silhouette is an outline of the train track. I took a new path this morning because the night before we had explored the vicinity of the Zeppelin Station and I discovered this station can lead me to the train. It's shorter. It was true it was shorter, but the elevator broke and I took four flights into the unknown. By then the city workers in their neon jackets had come out to make the madmen of trash less mad. My body felt heavy and torn between sleep and waking. My eyes were still adjusting to the new shadows that climbed the elevator shafts and the slanted light bouncing off the steps. I found a copper rotted wheel on the fourth stair of the station. It was vacant and empty like an old woman's belly.

By the time I took the escalator down into the bus station, the purplish Ff1 bus had poked its vernacular head into the station's tunnel and refused to turn its stubborn neck toward me as I ran half-heartedly after it.
I ran half-heartedly because my backpack bounced too much and it tired me in seconds and

because I needed to preserve my heartbeat and to diminish the pain that was gaining traction on the sleeves of my body, I left the bus to its dominant exit. I sat right down to read Daisuke Shen's "The Chariot Awaits." The story deals with suicide, betrayal, tarot cards, and the impossibility of loss.

On the bus, I thought of you in our warm bed. You would have been up already to shower and to brew coffee. Your neck would expose itself to light with a single brown claw hair clip. I thought of Cary Grant's proposal and the egg hatching theory that dominated their academic work. I wonder if you would forgive me for falling in love with our small rolls of toilet paper which has developed an intense, passionate relationship with my clitoris. I spend all day wiping iron off of me. You will read tonight. We each have a different way of turning our private mouths into reading machines. We also finished the last episode of Season 3 of *Manifest*. What will we occupy our minds with now

that the machine of Netflix
has abandoned us?

Maybe we'll watch Orphan
Black or the Hunters or the
Romanoffs? We'll eat shrimp
and my pork dish with the
corn you picked up and
maybe we'll try a new kind
of salt. The weekend will come
now and it will go, and you
think desire can dissolve
into my skin like the blot of
lotion you massage into the
crusted horseshoe of my
heel.

HELL CAN EXIST IN SOMEONE'S LEGS & TONIGHT THOSE LEGS ARE MINE

On our light gray elongated sofa, we watched the Jaguars fall to their jaguarian knees against the Bengals. I rooted & I rooted for Joe Burrow - who came from the south and not from wealth.

The last time Trevor Lawrence lost massively to Joe was when they played each other as Clemson vs LSU. I saw that game in my Vegas apartment after a Christmas holiday that left me sick for over a month.

I laid in my honeycombed mattress and stared at Joe's arms on the projected screen of my ceiling. Joe decimated Trevor both times. It must be quite an adjustment for Trevor who was 86-4 in high school and college and is now 0-4 in the NFL.

My father is losing his memory, too. He'd drive on Burlington into downtown to take me to the library and then forget at the stoplight to turn left or right. I think the mind is like the galaxy where things get expanded without our permission and wormholes appear where there shouldn't be.

our loved ones face intermittent amnesia. For us, who are still alive, amnesia doesn't dip its toes into the reservoir of memory.

It's a privilege for white thinkers to think that wisdom is overrated as often their acquired eventual "wisdom" arrives at the expense of colored folks. I tell you this.

In the elevator, I shifted the laundry in my arms to scan my fob, and I remembered being in college,

a key-card jammed in my back pocket and my arms full of books and I'd lean my hip into the sensor, and I remember feeling casually cool, and this afternoon I was thinking how, back then, my notion of coolness, chiselled my diction and movements down to

something jagged; a body in a casual lean.

We watched Tim Burton's Batman and I love how the Jo ker dances.

Your siblings & you wish your mother a happy birthday over ZOOM. She shares it with Jimmy Carter. You tell me she liked his policies.

The blue jumper the color of a cerulean sea that you thoughtfully purchased for me one early Denver afternoon remains in our closet.

It fits me perfectly - except its blue legs are too long and we must find a seamstress soon. My mother is one, but she doesn't believe in short legs and even if she did hem them, she'd make them so long I'd drag them like a wedding train down the sidewalks.

When Jack Nicholson's maniacal laughter disappeared from the black screen, you and I climbed into bed and made love. It seemed so long ago - when our bodies last touched that way.

The weight of my chronic pain kept our libido in the darkness. We made love, at first slowly. My body moved more latently - its erotic door appeared soft-spoken, delayed, and later it burst into some kind of accelerated, precipitated formlessness.

In the morning, you hopped quickly into the shower like a rabbit - I barely could make out your hind legs. Still, I remained in bed - angry at you - at how fast you hop. Underneath the cover, I breathed heavily and I tried to force myself to sleep.

Yesterday, we bought a swiffer & walked the aisles of the Asian Market. The air felt like fall and reminded me of somewhere I have once lived but I could not remember where. It surprised me, when I moved away from Buffalo, how hot August can be. I remember walking one fall in Athens Ohio to teach & the sticky wool skirt in heat felt all wrong for autumn. In Lafayette the air would sometimes, suddenly, bring back memories of my grandfather's blue truck. We bought a swiffer at Walmart & gifts at the Asian Market. The night before

I had a dream my dad died. One moment he was there and then he was gone. And my imagined grief gnawed on my gut all day like an obligation half-forgotten. In the evening we watched Prageeta get married on Zoom. Mike looked to me like Gregory Peck and Kazim's sweet joy was gently & adorable.

We ate baked tofu and drank Chardonnay, and for dessert we had sweet rice wrapped in banana leaves. In the evening, we watched the end of *I May Destroy You* and I think you did not like it. Perhaps, it was the meta-twist and the sequence of fantasies that involved murdering, supporting, and loving her rapist. If you think of it as a progression toward closure, she gains back power. Each scenario individually feels wrong. I sort of liked the meta-twist. The way each scenario became a different genre, each one more surreal than the one before. I loved the shock of Arabella showing the rapist under her bed, and that moment when, as viewers, we exist in a state of uncertainty-- the show twists out of the commonplace of laughter and assault and into a different genre.

I loved the scene when a pregnant Officer Beth enters the room followed by a pregnant Officer Funmi and Terry and Arabella take about 5 minutes to discuss getting pregnant together, then ask the Officers whether they will videotape each other's births, and Funmi's gentle professionalism, which involves a consistent lack of alarm, is taken slightly off guard, she begins to explain that it isn't the nature of their relationship to--but Terry quickly interjects you're not weird like us, and Funmi wears a slight smile. She's fond of them and her fondness is evident, like fresh creases in a starched shirt. I liked, too, that Terry ended up with a transman, and Kwame with a man who looks solid as a mountain.

We were not tired, and so, we watched the opening of *Batman Returns.*

I like Christopher Walkens hair, his icy white eyes, and purple suits.

I love how stylized this movie is. I love when

Walken shoves Pfieffer out his office window & she returns - 8/9ths alive - to her empty apartment and drinks milk straight from the carton, she

flips the switch on a lamp and it crashes to

the hardwood floor,

& the milk runs down her chin and blouse, a rivulet of blood running from her knuckles down her wrist and she runs back her messages: two calls from her mother and an ad for lady gotham perfume: one whiff of this at the office and your boss will be asking you to stay after work for a candlelit staff meeting

for   two,
which snaps
her   like   a
rubberband

'
- she breaks
a   doll
house,   a
phone,   the
neon "o" of
a sign that
brightly
says
"hello,"
with   a
frying pan -
and   when
the
wellspring
of   her
swallowed
screams   is
drained, she
arches   her
leather clad
back   and
meows.

When the Penguin tears
off his suit and returns
to the sewers, Danny
Elffman   knows   to

make the score both
haunting and tragic, but
we didn't get there yet. We got
tired and went to bed.

While you were deep asleep,
my body woke me up because
my   legs   were
uncooperative   and
unyieldingly in pain.

At 3 am I hung them
up like bats to alleviate
the throbbing pooling
in the bottoms of my
feet. I climbed back next to
you, but the pain returned.
This time more wretched
and obdurate.

At 4 am, I crawled
onto our long sofa and
hung my legs against
the giant windows. I
hung them for half an hour or
more while Twitter mocked
Urban Meyer, the head coach
of the Jaguars; who was caught
staunching the devastation of a
humiliating loss

with a young blonde grinding
at a bar. His wife, Shelley,
you reasoned must have

known this about his infidelity

It wasn't the first time a football player was promiscuous. I asked you if you'd leave someone caught cheating in that fashion. Your answer was practical, - you reasoned that that civic fornication is also a type of currency for the famous and the powerful.

They can't seem to live without it, you ratiocinate. At 5 am, I hung my legs again & I stood near our bed like a folded sofa, forcing pain to leak out of me through the pure force of unorthodox gymnastics. Meanwhile you slept like a phone inside of the phone booth.

When it rang and rang, you remained retro, vintaged, in your soporific, resilient bell system, disconnected from the modern world of my nocturnal corporeal chaos.

It's better, I reason, for one person to sleep well than for both to suffer at once. I splayed myself on the sofa to protect you from my body's anguished phone call. Hell can exist in someone's legs and tonight, it exists in mine.

BECAUSE I DO NOT WANT MEMORY TO BE A MYTH

For all I know, my brother could've been a vampire. But he drove a blue convertible, which he almost gave me and almost drove away from me & Marineland where we rode Dragon Mountain 20 times in a row & I told him we can scream, with impunity, in public & I love it.

I said, "Don't you love it, too?"

We fought that afternoon. At the funeral someone said, in half jest, "he loved Christmas." Was it true?

The New York Times Obituary called him a gay rights activist. Was that entirely accurate?

Alex was gentle & slender, a stranger, who told us my brother was the first man - besides lovers & family members - who he'd said *I love you* to & that seemed true, but, Alex, why had I never met you? Daphne read an excerpt from her memoir. She spoke of her depression & James, her personal assistant, who she'd find, frequently, asleep in one among her many bedrooms.

Because I do not want memory to be a myth, I become imperious

He struggled, too. He was a terrible house guest. That's true. Do you remember the scattered and half-packed suitcases all over the house? The ring of candy wrappers around the couch? Do you remember Chrisely Knows Best, My Strange Addiction, anything starring Queen Latifah? I crossed my arms over my chest, so privately proprietary, so vigilant, as if I stood to lose something else.

Do you remember all the suitcases he brought to Key West? Do you remember the one he'd filled with every color of boat shoes?

Daphne said his novel was brilliant & unfinished & I knew nothing of it. In high school, he made Channah so mad she kicked him out of her house (with her leg!). Jill said *The Red Fern* made her cry in 5th grade, and the new boy, whose desk was beside hers, touched her shoulder and told her he was sad, too. I had not known so much. Shruti said she would not be herself without his friendship & yes, he was a terrible house guest. We shared a room, and by the time I'd arrived home for the holiday, he'd eaten snacks in both our beds. His grandfather died hiding complementary apples under his mattress. He was rear-ended, by an hysterical kid, who'd intended to hijack his car. Jim fed him snacks and they waited in the cool interior of his blue convertible. He once fell into razor wire. God knows why. He crashed his motorcycle in the rain, while driving down a winding mountainside. He called once from the parking lot of a motorcycle safety class. He'd gone inside and come back out because the other men were heavy-set & dressed in fatigues

& bandanas. They had ponytails & tattoos. "You know the type I'm describing, right?" He said. He had an olive multi-pocket army jacket in the trunk of his car. "Should I put it on?"

I am tempted to say I sent care packages to Delhi. I don't remember sending anything. My mother sent packages my brother paid bribes to receive. Why would the ashes be his? The air in Delhi was thick with smoke and ash. I saw it on Democracy Now. How odd to think. Does it matter whose ashes they sent? I loved a person and what is a person?

I owed him a phone call. Laura said he sounded

lucid. Because he had not died yet, I thought he'd live.

I said I'd tell Sally she lived in our childhood neighborhood her kids had all gone off to college. She taught Jim gardening and origami & she called him her friend. Back then, he preferred grown women to boys who pulled him by the legs from minivans where he'd hide from them. I asked Sally to tell me a story about Jim. I said, what do you remember? At the funeral, my mother said he'd always been a gentle boy & it was true. And Laura - whose stories always made me laugh - sobbed, unexpectedly, into my hair before flying back to Los Angeles. When John left New York he gave me his heavy oak desk and when I left I stuffed the drawers with candy &

gave the desk to Jim. This must have been 2008 & on a gritty August day, Laura sat on the desktop on the Crown Heights sidewalk & said, *when I think of candy, I think of Jim & when I think of Jim, I think of candy.*

Back then, we always wound up kissing on Jim's balcony midway through every one of his posh parties, which reminded me of Madmen. It may have been the cocktail shaker, the gin, or the stainless steel strainer. On my birthday, Jim took me to see Jill Sobule sing in a large dark piano bar with blue lights and velvet seat covers & Laura met us at a bistro in the East Village, with bronze ceiling tiles, & I drank wine & watched them banter, which I loved & then he tucked me in a cab & paid the fare. Or maybe it's Fitzgerald's "Winter Dreams": that middle class boy eternally reaching for glittering things. He took me to a rooftop party in Boerum Hill, the neighborhood where I foamed cream for people's lattes, but could not afford to live. I don't remember the rooftop, only the sidewalks in that part of Brooklyn are brick and dappled in sunlight and the trees are sometimes big. We went for his friend, Olivia - who, ten years later, would ship him a ventilator and oxygen - but that night she was waiting for an ex named Hugh to take her home with him & Jim wanted to be there if he didn't. At 4AM, this sandy-haired rascal in nantucket reds stumbled, smirking onto the rooftop. I think, in fact, I'd heard him coming, shouting, just to hear himself, down the block, up the steps, and onto the rooftop. Imagine waiting for that! Jim had brought a bottle of Skyy Vodka, which he stuffed in my bag on the way out. He lived in Harlem, then, & so, we took a cab to my apartment and I said Olivia is too good for Hugh, and Jim smiled at me and said, isn't he awful? That night, we passed out in my twin bed, and he wrapped his arms around my waist, and I had not known he held people in his sleep, & I had not known he'd want to hold me. That morning when I arrived late to work, my boss, Patrick, took my bag from my shoulder & said "This is awfully heavy, Jess?" & pulled out the bottle of Skyy vodka, to my surprise!, & we laughed.

Remember when I balanced a glass of water atop his bedroom door? I called him in & water drenched his hair & shirt & he was delighted. I think he had a liquor cabinet on wheels & a silver bucket full of ice. I think his friends wore suits to his parties. And at the funeral, when Laura cried into my hair, I said goodbye, I love you and it was true.

That morning, my phone ringing, silently on the windowsill, while I was sleeping, still believing I'd need a good night's sleep.

Will you miss singing in hotel lobbies? Meeting my handsome friends–Joshua and John–and flirting shamelessly with them? Will you miss crushing on our sister's husbands? And how the second one was wounded when you said you'd crushed on the first one, too? Telling me to stop making out with your best friend, Laura? How I promised but I could not stop? We were so young then. Standing in a parking lot? Holding a badly packed grocery bag? Stopping in a stairwell to catch your breath? Will you miss roller coasters and laughing inside elevators? Or talking yourself into things, like waking? Looking out a window at rain. Your anger. What have you done with it? Thinking something, such as, Under every myth is a truth too difficult–believing you have finally figured it out– then wondering whether you've only arrived at a different myth?

On the evening drive to Boulder it took longer than usual for the crisp outline of mountains to come into focus.

Do you remember trolling Gayatri Spivak for an autograph and I was horrified but feigned delight? The last time we spoke, you called at 7AM, my time, to ask if I'd ever wasted a perfectly good joke on an audience who didn't get it.

Yes! I said, I had. In fact, I was just talking about that!

You said you knew I'd understand.

A DEED CAVE CALLED SLEEP

When I climbed the platform to the train your words returned like a plastic bag fluttering in debris. You said, Zverev moves like a clumsy pelican. We both wanted Novak to make history but more than this we did not want Alexander - the beach blond with a penchant for choking women and ordering them to die *outside* his hotel suite - to win. Your pork sat in the rubbery belly of my packed lunch whose sky was full of herbaceous sesame oil and seeds, which could not cross-pollinate with my heavy breathing.

While waiting for the bus to come, I struggled to expel my

breath. My heart ached with bone-deep pain. The bus rolled into the city like a diva's carpet and when I climbed on it, a woman with pink hair apologized while taking the seat beside mine. I wanted to breathe. I stowed my navy bag on the adjacent seat and gazed into the empyrean sky that fused Denver with Boulder for the answer to my continual existence.

The bus driver apologized profusely at Broadway and Euclid. He didn't know how to fold back the legs to the ramp. He kicked and kicked the handicap door like a piece of rock that would not budge. I remember, yes, your nocturnal hands and your naked chest. In the morning, your breath has the specific soporific scent of a woody husk and I yearned to stay where I was.

You promised to deliberate my concupiscent appetite with the slow, deft seasoning of your tongue. I couldn't help but feel morose in my office as I read Godard's last novel. And I wondered if you had re-parked the car and carried our jasmine rice up four floors to our apartment.

Today, Denver is breathing sand. Zverev's father probably abuses him and your enthusiasm for Djokivic faded when he said Zverev was a good guy on and off the court. Besides, last night, your body was a tiny furnace radiating warmth.

You texted to say you'd come to the station and carry my navy bag home for me. Even knowing this ahead, I was startled when the elevator doors flashed open - & there you were, in sepia-striped slacks, standing in a slanted fashion like you were about to start a 50 meter dash. At the far end of the pedestrian bridge, a young guy with a skateboard tried keeping pace with a woman who walked, quickly, away from him, her eyes lowered to the ground.

You did not turn to watch but I could tell that you were listening. You whispered to me and, suddenly, without thinking, we stepped into the elevator with them.

The man, holding a skateboard in one arm, gripped her neck tight, and would not let go. We chaperoned her to the platform and waited for her train to come. He stood on the steps and shouted at the tracks. *Stupid. Bitch. Come back.* Her back was bulgy black like a humpback. She lit a cigarette, took two puffs, soberly and faintly squashed its flickering volcanic head between

her thumb and index finger before climbing into the moratorium of the train which arrived in a halting fashion, suctioning wind inwards

45

before exhaling like a chronic smoker near our standing feet. We descended a flight of stairs before I turned my head back to let the other two passengers know that there was vomit, from a dog or human, ahead. You had accomplished so much in a day: two loads of laundry, sink washing, teaching two courses. You even had time to carry our child, this 25 pound bag of Jasmine rice - into our apartment, you re-parked our Subaru, and you bought eggs and coffee.

You'd been distracted, listening over your shoulder, at the couple standing outside the elevator doors. I asked how your day was. You whispered, hold on. It's just, you said, that man. He won't leave that woman alone. You'd seen them in the elevator already. The door opened and the angle of their bodies was so convert and revelatory, you felt as though you'd crawled into a stranger's bed and you apologized and let the doors close on them again and took the steps up to the pedestrian bridge. And when you arrived she was stepping out of the elevator and he was gripping the back of her neck and telling her they'd work it out. They'd work it out. Her shoulders slumped, her neck looked stooped and so defeated, and when she pulled away, his tone changed.

I am stubborn. So stubborn, you said. Stubborn as a small stone wall. He saw it, you said. I'd act like a whack-a-mole, impassively, pop back up again, if I was knocked down. And, so, eventually, he walked off and stopped on the steps and shouted down at the tracks. *Stupid. Bitch. Come back.* Her back was bulgy black like a humpback. A turtle. Tucked up before a blow. She said, "He'll never stop." She said, "Thank you." She almost smiled. She lit a cigarette, took two puffs, soberly and faintly squashed its flickering volcanic head between her thumb and index finger before climbing into the moratorium of the train. You almost touched her shoulder before she left. You almost asked whether she wanted him to come back.

I was profoundly tired and my chest ached. It surprised you that in spite of this I put my body between them. You hung your legs that night against the bamboo-style bedpost beside me. You wanted to share in my routine, but felt only the mollifying pain of ritual. You wished I had a pain free life.

That's called death, I said *and y*ou disagreed. Death isn't life you said and repeated yourself, knocking each word out - like a mallet sounding out the hollowness of a wall. And you laughed a wild laugh. Why does this sound nearly orphic? you asked.

YOU MET DEATH ON LEX

and asked her to meet you at a hotel in Brooklyn You would not meet her in Vegas where the sounds of your mother's movements came through the walls between your rooms. Meanwhile, in another state Death courted our brothers on Uber and Grinder As you removed one blind eye from the invisible pocket of your black bra You realized that your memory of your brother had an invisible purse With its zipper sewn on its side and its contents were pennies or wishes So when they hit the surface of your eye the world you knew rippledBack then all you wanted was a plate of black olives impaled by toothpicks charred from a wild fire that raged Northern California

In winter, you wanted a fireplace, too, and a thick soup you weren't allergic to. During autumn rain the earthworm on your sternum writhed
& you were deciding whether to die or live your life wedded to Zinfandel's fading legs or to walk through an inch of snow to buy three mangosteens from a corner grocery store
Back when I knew none of this and knew you less, I climbed wet stairwells, snowflakes melted on

my eyelashes, and clumps of snow fell off the trees, which were heavy and shaggy and white and green I pulled myself close beneath my heavy coat and the train I got on began moving in and out of the elongated, silvery body of an eel while the conductor spoke through his amplified microphone attached like a second, semi-translucent, chain-mail-like skin, "Do you need anything? Say chocolate?" And, the trainy eel obediently responded, which surprised you greatly, "The compressor in me is broken.

It's like the heart of the AC and, no, all I need is a new shoulder, honey."
As if the train seat had been a bassinet, the engine a chimney
coughing up clouds, I knew that I would drift off in smoke and for another year
Or two I'd doze. Back then I told everyone
My favorite thing about Pennsylvania is leaving Pennsylvania on a train.
Especially after Clarice Lispector spit black tobacco into a tin can and left it
near the railing. I have always known this about love: the ground you
place it on does not exist. I knew, too, that sleep is not a type of aonair

wine, situated above my consciousness, waiting for their insomnia of volcanic
ash to make me drift like a listless soul. Beneath that Lispector phlegm, that thick
oral mucus, hint of smoke and ash, was an answer to a question I had not yet learned to ask.

So, all the way to Brooklyn, I slept. The train rocked my body back and forth
like a jug of water inside of a stroller. From the window view, the effervescent
trees were woefully mourning their winter-torn sleeves, standing tall and hip-wide
like pregnant women in a dream, I exited the train, and climbed the stairs to your hotel room,
where you lay on your back begging Death to let you sleep on the railroad track
or take pesticides in the countryside with South Korea. The winter had been
long and wet and when, in a dream's sunset, I crept up the steps, I like to
think Death heard what you could not hear yet,
because she startled and she left and the sun spread, warm and diluted, on
the backs of my eyelids and I woke just as the train screamed into Penn
Station's open mouth. With the grayish duffel bag strapped over my left shoulder,
I lowered and bowed my head while my feet slowly marched
through the crowd's soporific mourning of procession.
Each human head was a dark blue, wilted tulip, its witless petals drooped
and sagged heavily against the gullible sound of footsteps amplifying and

triangulating the proximity of my distance. I
shoveled along the cylindrical
cement walls, into the yellow glow of a
stairwell, and stepped up just as the
sun set on Vernon Boulevard.

Meanwhile, on the other
side of Pulaski Bridge,
maybe 40 minutes
walking distance, you
sobbed intermittently
into a grocery bag which
waved
like a half-staffed,
mortified flag in the
wind, & eventually it
floated away from you
as you stopped at the
corner of Nassau where
clumps of sooty snow
had
melted and frozen again
and the walk sign flashed
white and you crossed
the avenue just like the
living do. The short walk
was the longest walk you
ever took
in your very short life --
the compelling wind was
pushing you and you
like
a pregnant woman,
pushing you towards the
metro, pushing you into
the pavement,
pushing you into the
snow. By then it was
night and I stood beside a
giant window
on the 21st floor of 474
48th Avenue watching
the empire state building

change color. The black sky was perforated with a thousand tiny squares
of light, each one ushering me, like a Russian novel, into its own domestic
tragedy : a tv glowing in a living room, a couple eating take out at a kitchen
counter, a man smoked on a narrow balcony and curled himself against the wind.
To stand beyond the reach of weather, I discovered, was yet another
way I may be lonely. It was all emptiness, staring into the private things that
couldn't stare back at me. Sometimes the intimacy of distance
was too much. The glasses on the ridge of my nose refused to be that lonely
rose, fading, wilting from that indeterminate breath that had fogged up their glass.
I took the elevator down 21 flights to the street where black cabs stood
waiting and a driver asked if he was waiting for me. I assumed no one was and I crossed the street. At that point, I had met you twice.

Once I took an Uber to a
restaurant where clavicles
were juxtaposed
between wooden and
metal chairs shifting in
and out of periphery, but
your clavicle was most
prominent of all. You sat
diagonally from me,
silently
sipping hot water with a
wedge of lemon, your
fingers spread with
gentle
strength around the
teacup's opening. You
ordered salmon and ate
slowly
with your eyes shyly
downcast. For a moment,
I sat inside the soft light
of
your quiet pleasure, the
setting sun lit the wooden
table and glowed
against your profile. You
squinted slightly, and
delicately speared small
flakes of
salmon. You hardly
spoke save when
someone said I was
adorable, and you shyly
raised your eyes to mine
and you agreed. When
you left, the place
you sat was stainless and
the sun fell behind you,
leaving the city in a
dismal neglect of chance.
I, however, collected
myself and you placed
me

in a box called Wisdom. I
waited by the light for life
to change her colors
from infancy to myopia.
You waited and waited
for the city to change
what we were unable to
change until four years
into the future. That
evening,
sitting with my legs
curled up by the hotel
bed, I thought
about my brother, Jim,
who had a way of holding
me tight in
his arms when we slept.
Years later, when he took
a large bubble
bath full of foam in India,
I kept on having a
recurring dream of Jim
dying and of having to
announce the devastating
news to new people
each night.

We met, the first time,
inside a crowded
convention
center. Djuna Barnes,
famous fictionist, wore a
cowboy hat. She stood
several rows from me,
and laughed with such
exquisite abandon. By
contrast,
you stood patient as the
sunlight, and I leaned
toward your
warmth the way some
plants twist out of shade.
I have always

been so reticent in the
company of others, my
sapphic shyness
peeling out of me like a
clementine in front of a
bay of unripe avocados
or
overripe raspberries. You
gave me chocolate and
two books and later, the
next day or the day after
that, I could not stop
crying while I waited for
my
train to come and take me
back.
Four years ago, in that
endless   Pennsylvania
winter,
I wrote you, "All I do is
grade papers but I have a
fold out."
It was a faceless message,
the kind written in the
quiet, iridescent
recess of my idleness, the
kind that arrived after a
storm has been built
right into the towering
headdress of a tornado,
the kind that walked
out of you like a vagrant
beggar from a beach
house near the
sea. When I
was young, I coped with
my queerness, my
handsome isolation, my
overwrought
loneliness by smoking
weed, one string of
vaporous vapor
ornamentation after

another, by the window
and climbing
through it after dark. My
body was strikingly
vigorous, though I spent
most of its innocent
muscularity by being
restlessly listless,
walking in
and out of kitchen doors
like I knew the
difference between
having a
wallet and David Foster
Wallace.

You were reticent and precise.
The wind
blew into a window and the
stacks of papers before each
paid
grader swirled around the
room, save yours, which you
held down
with your free hand, while
tapping your sharpened pencil
against the tabletop. The others,
limp and languid like
overwatered
houseplants, shuffled listlessly
between the window and the
vending
machine. You did not hear
them. Your focus was
unparalleled, your eyes
scanned the page, you made a
swift mark, and moved on.
They nudged
their papers to your side of the
table. I cannot help but picture
them: boorish
brothers and grinning
stepsisters, turning the key in
the lock, and leaving. You

did not notice. You turned the
page, and tapped your pencil
against
the tabletop. Then it was five
o'clock, a winter night. The
castrated
photographer pushed his bike
over the ice and up the rolling
hills and past the frosted
cornfields to your door. I
wonder what it was like
to say goodnight. Your profile,
your steady eyes fixed on the
horizon,
and your silence, while he
confessed he'd like to dip his
fist into your head.
He said it would come out
sweet and soaked in golden
honey. He painted you a
blurry
picture of yourself. Your wrist
bone bent oddly to the left. He
had a sheep's head
shipped to you from Morocco
and a Nordic Wolffish from the
Arctic Circle.
He wrote a sonnet each day and
sent them in a box he'd carved
from
whale bone inside a box made
of glue and pigeon's nests. You
did not
know what to do with all of
these intoxicated gifts. You
could not carry
them around and so you bought
a plastic storage box, folded
each gift neatly into scented
tissue paper and closed the lid. I
wrote
you in Pennsylvania. I said, "I
have a fold out," then I put on

my headphones and spent the
evening walking under the
yellow
glow of street lamps, the red
brick, the sparkling snow. That
was
not the same year. I walked like
a downcast philosopher
beneath the Kinzua Bridge,
measuring my time and distance
slowly. All of
my vacant thoughts were in the
clouds, waiting for the
precipitation of a long lost
meaty memory of meeting a
future
you to rain back down to me,
storming my petite form into
an
ambulated oblivion. My life has
been this long, arduous
academic road.
My head always in the dense
pages. Those long endless
paragraphs
where the wheat, the cornfield,
and the muted stone of an idea
traveled
back and forth between
prolixity and nothingness.

From time to time, I
wonder if you would marry me
even after our galaxy stopped
expanding. I wonder on nights
like this if you would mutely
climb
inside my submarine and sit
beside me until all the speed
boats sped
past. I wanted to walk beside
you up a narrow stairwell with
arms full

of paper bags and rice and cabbage and keys jangling in your hand. I

wondered whether you'd love me more if we fell onto the bed or

if instead I scrubbed the crisper down before dumping the vegetables in, or

whether you'd forgive me if I slept and the sound of engines carried

my dream to the beach and if a smog curtain closed behind me and if I

went on wondering whether you liked wrist bones or clavicles best, or if I

went on wanting, in spite of it, to fold my mouth around your hip, would you know?

Would you hold my face in your hands like a melon and carry my head home?

We'd hardly met. I was learning so many words do not mean what

I thought they did. I have come to understand moisture in a very different

way. Words often, despite my heavy proclivity for wanting them to, do not

have much moisture in them. They lack water and something else.

Something I can't pin my fingers on. Something to do with acoustic

signals or density or the waxy content in the cranium of dolphins. After

reaching into my armpits in the
dark afternoon many years later
for

two wheats and three stones, I
found your fingers cracking
out laughing

like they heard a terrible knock
knock joke from the edge of
their

alpha-keratin. I wonder if you
would love me less if all my
clocks and

obligations cracked wide open
and I oozed out, formless as
raw egg or if I

was not ticklish or if I owned an
orange cat. The kind that spoke
Cantonese

or Vietnamese with a Southern
drawl. The kind that a mandarin
orange

would mistake for its distant,
house-arrested cousin. Some
mornings

when I woke up in the early
light to unlower the blinds,

the kind that made you more
sultry and less formal in the
Houston

darkness, I imagined you being
a fruit basket that someone

accidentally left on the third
floor of a vacant apartment
complex. There

were bell peppers that didn't
shake like bells and there were
mythologies

in you that didn't arrive with a
broken chariot on its coeval
asphalt.

In times like these, you don't
ever take the elevator with me
to the rooftop

with the lavish bar and
flamboyant cocktails that night
we ordered
cabernet and sunk into the
plush cushions and did not
drink a sip of it and I felt
as if I'd stepped inside a future
where I did not exist or a
memory that
belonged entirely to someone
else. The night was all around
us and, for
an instant, I was certain it was
me and not my brother who
was dead.
But in the morning when I
raised the blinds
your stillness, which is either
that of a hummingbird
or its opposite, is so exquisitely
composite and fatalistic and so
I try hard to step inside of it. A
fantasy you once told me.
I lean over you. I brush your
cheek. My neck crowned by
a collar of trees. I say, *Baby,
how did you sleep?*

I slept poorly and
unevenly   -   like   my
subconsciousness sat on an old
fashioned
scale - the owlgift vintage - the
kind that represents truth and
fairness. But
on the other side, the other side
of your amnesia, the one you
had only
known   briefly   and
intermittently,   the   one
outweighing everything
about the rapid heartbeats of
raven who sat (unevenly) on an
old redwood

tree by the side of road.
Compelled by distance and
sadness, I swiftly cup
your face like an old beggar
cleaning knives for the
endangered denizens
of the foggy city he dreams up
each night then watches swirl
slowly
down the drain of each
morning, leaving his belly full
of a
sadness that is jagged and
undefined. It is possible,
of course, to miss someone who
sleeps beside you, too,
and so I remove a hybrid
hyacinth from a drawer of a
tree and whisper soporific
leaves into it so that it is always
falling asleep by exfoliating into
what you always
love and can love. There is a
mist waiting outside like a
widow.
Her eyes are soft and wet with
tears or sweat from running up
an evanescent hill. I try to run
my hands through her near the
mulberry
well as a way of telling you that
I wish your heartbeat smelled
like a tea
kettle with fresh mint stuck in
its sprout: metallic and fresh
and blooming
with an arc of wheat. Longing
so thick makes my hands
somnolent, even my knuckles
lull the handle of a
teakettle to sleep. In your
absence, I pour hot water up
into

a mug, with a wedge of lemon
and take the steam into myself
as if I were pulling on your
breath.   Meanwhile,   a
livestream
of the Governor's address
drones on in the background, I
sigh
into a kitchen that is newly
emptied of you and the kettle
sighs,
too, and the governor says it's
impossible   to   quantify
suffering.
But I have drifted to a time long
before Ida or Covid-19, I am
rousing my Manhattan bound
self from a dream,
and pulling her by her winter
sleeves, up the endless steps
of a Brooklyn hotel, ordering
death to leave.

YOUR SILENCE HAS THE LANDMASS OF QUEBEC

In the aftermath of an argument, your silence has the landmass of Quebec and neighboring provinces such as Prince Edward and New Brunswick. In the earliest morning hours of our waking, you brushed the tips of my fingers with your clement, quiet lips. I wanted to smother you in the darkness of my dreaming.

Instead I climbed out of the benevolent circumference of your tenderness, and forced the showerhead to ache rainwater. I stood under it. By the time I departed our Blueground apartment, I had already sent your deodorant flying and crashing onto our vanity sink. I had already opened and closed too many closet doors. And, in the blank darkness, the space between the large mirror and our bathroom, you asked if my office was even open on a Sunday.

I didn't care. Even when I stood on the platform while the train screeched into the station, I thought of your gaze and of how **I longed for your morning breath to re-wake me into another day.** A day filled with the noise you would make when you learned Emma Raducanu shocked the world with her unpredictable groundstrokes & won the US Open.

I climbed the platform to wait for the train and your words returned to me like a grocery bag fluttering in the debris. You said Alexander Zverev moved like a clumsy pelican. He lost - thank god! - to Djokovic. We both wanted Novak to make history. I thought of your pork sitting in the rubbery belly of my packed lunch whose sky was filled with the herbaceous sesame oil and seeds which couldn't cross-pollinate with my heavy breathing.

I waited for the Boulder Ff1 bus to come. My heart ached with bone-deep pain and the bus rolled into the city like a diva onto a diva carpet. When I climbed on it, a woman with pink hair apologized for taking the seat beside me. I wanted so badly to breathe. As in I wanted to expire. I'd stowed my navy bag on the adjacent seat to keep someone from taking it. I kept gazing into the empyrean sky that fused Denver with Boulder for the answer to my continual existence.

The driver apologized profusely, at Broadway and Euclid, for making us late. He didn't know how to fold up the legs of the ramp. He kept kicking the handicap door like a piece of rock that would not budge. I remember, yes, your nocturnal hands and naked chest were glazed wet like sticky rice. And, how your entire body was like grated copra and coir in the obedient dark. In the morning, your breath has the specific soporific scent of a woody husk and I yearned to stay where I was.

Monday felt like Sunday. The sun sliced the blinds with blades of light. At the Asian Market, I moved, frenetically, through the aisles. I wanted to show you how big a jackfruit is, to feed you Chè Chuối from a spoon, and bánh cam, which is hard to find and harder to make. I bought mung bean, Bột Khoai, Bột bán, ginger candy, and two kinds of coconut juice. You bought a bag of jasmine rice the size of a small child. In the car you ate a hole into the bánh cam so I could eat the mung bean out. In the late afternoon you read a story about Rick and Carol, who drank too much of a strange cocktail and forgot who they were. *In the mountains, you feel free.* Our meal that night was multi-colored: red rice, purple cabbage, pork and green onions. You were impatient to climb into bed beside me. I was anxious about your car outside. You kissed my eyebrows and eyelids, the bridge of my nose, my cheekbones. My pain had slightly subsided.

It never did feel like Monday and so suddenly it was the next day. 3:45AM and I am whispering. You said, 'baby, go back to bed," and I did, and then it was morning again, and I pulled my black jumpsuit with the white polka dots onto my body. I leaned over you, my hair still wet. I said, "I can't wait to come back home again."

It was Tuesday and soon it would be Wednesday and Thursday and then Friday again. I stood on the platform in the chill of 5AM with the cranes and train bells and silos in the distance. I'd told you in the logic of half sleep

we ought not to make the air so cool at night. We wake in cold sweat. We throw the blankets off ourselves and our perspiration turns to ice. I'd told you life is so short, Jess.

LIGHT LIKE

ELEPHA NTS

Inspired by our co-meditation, I led my Fiction and Poetry sections into 10 minutes of silence. I feel for them: their restlessness and exhaustion. A young poetry student breathlessly flew into class. She had just climbed four flights of stairs. Another student asked if she could close the blinds. Light floated into the room like elephant ears, flapping lightly as if they were listening, wanting to be the beat poets too like Ginsberg or Lucien Carr or Leonard Cohen. They, my students that is, were blissful about the weather: sunless, morose, dark clouds like fat sacks of scrotum, waiting to burst their seams or semen open. My toes remained wet and hiemal and benumbed while I ate chicken and rice in my office.

I met a young man over Zoom who went to West Point and talked about his unreluctant appetite for Africa. I await with great anticipation our Zeppelin Station date tonight with a glass of wine, skee-ball, and pac-man. You enjoy watching these postmodern creatures with voracious mouths consuming ghosts and yellow pellets. Perhaps you have an addictive personality after all. For a long time, I thought perhaps you were one of those accented things that dependency and enslavement couldn't meet. Whenever we are shopping time with arcade games, you glow like a rhubarb pie. And, each time, my love for you grows and grows like fleshly thickened rhizomes. It only makes you even more tart and ever more interesting. Meanwhile in class, my brother texted me. He asked me, "Where do you want the $400?" I quickly replied, "US Bank or Venmo." My heart leaps out of my chest whenever he texts me. Especially if he addresses me by my name. I miss him all the time now - wondering if Ubering has been kind to him. I wonder if he has been taking his heart medications and if he is eating well. Or if he has found a different way to commit suicide. To die. I spoke to you twice on the phone before you arrived to collect me. One to ask you to alter your Southwest flight from Providence to Denver. It was 29 dollars cheaper and why not? And, the other, to address our vanity drawer, our fire alarm, and our vanity sink that continues to smell intensely of sulfur. We had been contacting Blueground, on and off, for about 27 days now about that and they remained slipshod, negligent. I wonder if it would help our cause if we wrote Blueground a review everyday of their blatant mercenary oscitation until they repair our loft to the ideal condition we so desire.

When I walked out of Hellem to meet you, 4 young men in blue suits & fancy loafers & flushed cheeks walked past me. Their shoulders were hunched over.

I very nearly ran over them. Those boys in blue suits & floppy blond hairdos. They looked exhilarated. That crosswalk creeps out of the trees and the turn into the parking lot is sharp. You stood in the parking spot & I nearly pulled into it; flanked by two large trucks--a dangerous choice, Vi Khi Nao. I nearly ran over you, too! That night we joined Zoom and listened to Prageeta Sharma talk about anticipatory grieving.

My father forgets. He was, at one time, so highly dependable, but I am learning now that he cannot be depended upon to remember anymore. He walks into a room and forgets why he entered it. Most of the time he looks confused, and knocks curled fingers against his temple.

About a year ago, my brother, Jim, told me he had a lot of experience with dead fathers and when I was ready to talk about my father's declining health he'd be there. But I did not want to talk about it. I was in a rush to get someplace & the conversation felt forced, & besides he'd misunderstood my response. It wasn't denial. I was wondering why - just when I began to feel for myself - I had to feel sorry for him, again?

When we play pac-man, you always win the most rounds, and I always eat the most. I tell you on the way home, as we walk in and out of the yellow orbs of light that fall in spheres on the rocky grey street, that you focus on survival and I focus on pleasure. In Rhino, we can pour a glass of wine into a plastic cup, and walk home arm and arm in the middle of the empty road. There are fences and weeds growing somehow out of gravel and the lights are glowing in the distance. You say, 'it's ironic, isn't it? For someone who doesn't want to live?"

I AM ASKING YOU TO BUILD A CITY WITH ME

In the morning of my heaviness, the smoke from the fire drifts in and out of the coffee mug of the city. You keep on pouring and pouring the bedstraw family out of my body, wanting the psyche to dissolve. My heart is beating not hard against my chest. No drum resonance. No coffee creamer that would yield slender sleeves from its white flower. I gazed at you in my sleep. It was a sleep of urine and condensation. My body is herbaceous - not in the botanical sense - just gin on fire by its roots and shrubs. Semi-circular in its fumigation, the skirt of ferns and grasses are growing into straw and stone. Do you still want to build a city?

Here the roads are poorly paved. An egret flies low across a highway. Black pavement turns to black lake; the trucks cough up dull clouds and vanish behind buildings. The sky is a sock turned inside out, it flops over the skyline and throws up. Meanwhile, at the regional airport, a well-dressed city with healthy boundaries, orders a latte. I'll call you, it says into an i-phone, when I get home. And thus, the festivals all come to their hurried end and hurricane season begins.

With higher elevation, the air is thick. Though not with indigestion. The light fell asleep when you took an Uber to the grocery store. In your grocery bag, there were a dozen free range eggs, pregnant with western Texas. The mountains here are layers of silhouettes and you sit in your sadness as the rice finishes cooking itself over an electric stove whose smoke has the same bold texture as fire in the Bay Area. You forgo anger and denial and go straight to sorrow, which is to say, you are quick to accept.

People have diarrhea all the time: the city that smokes itself. I run my fingers over the edge of my melancholy while the earth shakes its hip and leaves so many people to die in the belly of Haiti. Are earthquakes a way in which the tree takes a sabbatical from dry mud? When you climbed into bed that evening, the evening you arrived in Boulder, I thought the pregnant chicken had cut off its own head. You wanted to sleep the deep sleep. The kind that one never wakes up from. The one that leaves me behind. In a cargo made for a driftless soul. The kind that was idyllic and restful. And, so I imagine a city in which the buses run in trapezoidal circles and a bicycle rack in which I could stash my love.

When I worked for a bed and breakfast as a linen cleaner, I used to make the beds so fast that I could devote my afternoons to reading. I left you all alone. I felt the agony of your departure. I thought hard about a noisy bird that sang to you. I thought hard about staying in Louisiana in the fall, to live a soft, innocent life, where the deep exhaustion keeps my heat and body moisture at bay. I tried so hard to please you. I do the things you ask. I planned Dallas and West Texas for us. And, I often tell you that I love you.

The kind of love that mixes sweat with hair. The kind of love that resides in the forehead. I tell you all these things while I agonize and you take an Uber.

And so, I waited and you sat silent and pensive on the other end. Your life tumbling into green hills, and blue skies from an uber window that curved like domes or slopped rooftops--you said don't worry, I am thinking of everything. You cast your eyes to the horizon and I waited. I imagined you, eternally wheeling your luggage into Baltimore's lampless streets, the light broken or blinking, and under the phone wires, the figure of another woman, sagging slowly into the sidewalk.

Like a cloud, you collect the folds of your mind's dress, and hover, quietly, over the bed. Your brow casts its shadow on the teal blue backboard and the grey comforter, where weeks ago you turned your arms to ropes and tied me to yourself. After all this, a suitcase meticulously packs itself.

And, of course, I know there is a before. One lover to lift the boulder off your back, and another to lead you through the maze of a cityscape and give you tea to sleep. And Calvino, who drove hours and hours through a sweltering Las Vegas sunrise, big balls of sweat rolling down his forehead. Your reticence is the lingering perfume in an elevator that has long been empty. How do you tell me this gently, that you have gone already?

I tried to hold myself like a parasol or a sack or a question mark to lay over the lobe of your left ear. I tried, didn't I? But I needed, too, to extinguish this exhaustion, which climbed the elevator of my soul, the escalator of my limbs, the stairwell of my ribs and prevented me from lingering next to your embrace. Every eye is a door. Every z is a lock. And so I slept and locked my mind inside itself. And, inside of this cryptic monochrome of my imprisonment, I realized that I wanted very much to let down my hair for you. Not necessarily one strand at a time, maybe two strands and a few eyelashes.

So, I ran - my face, my eyebrows, even my nostrils were soaked in sweat. I texted you a photograph, a selfie, of my temporary diaphoresis, letting you know that I could be a defiant and casual portrait of sultry and I could be inexcusably scandalous too. I ran my hands through my hair as I showered and I thought of you. Of your shyness and frenziness the day I drove into Iowa City with my maroon Subaru, the kind that lesbians drive to campsites. In Iowa, you showed me the driveway. I cupped your face, and you hurried across beige light into the house and up the steps, here you said is the closet, and here is a nightstand and here is a typewriter, you said. And in the typewriter there was a letter, it said: welcome home, Jess. And you said, here, there is your towel, and here are some snacks, and I laughed and carried you to the bed.

Sometime in the future of this moment, while you were far away, very close to Denver, though closer to Boulder, while sitting in an Uber car heading away from the Museum of Natural History, you emailed me a review in its draft form of your most recent Airbnb experience: "I was lured in, unfortunately, by this Airbnb's excellent reviews, but I will admit you get what you pay for which was my own misjudgment and oversight. I believe the host, Judy, is the property manager, Adam. It was a smart move on Adam's part because I wouldn't have booked it if I knew a man was Airbnbing his extra space in his living room for an additional source of income and using a woman's name Judy as a front . I was woken up at 5 in the morning each morning of my mid-stay - I left early and booked another Airbnb because of the early morning noises of Adam taking his dog out and I couldn't go back to sleep. Plus, I could hear the water running, Adam's footsteps and Adam's dog's paw steps. I could hear Adam's hands shuffling into a big bag to retrieve dog food for his dog. All of this inevitably disturbed my peace and sleep. On top of this, the flimsy partition gives no privacy -though I acknowledge the attempt was somewhat made. Had I known the other room with closed door was available for $3 more I would have taken it. Also, I woke up with a trail of insect bites on my legs and ankles. It worried me greatly. Also, the toilet was what is the word - reminds me of toilets at gas stations....The bathroom was clean, but at the same time, it wasn't."

The dog paced the floors of that strange house, and you slept, I think, like a roach, strangely in a strange home, hopping out of the light they lived inside, sleeping on the other side of a thin and semi-transparent partition. And I ran that night in the rain and the lightning cracked and I ran beneath the magnolia trees. Slick streets. Slick grass. Clouds drifted over the mall parking lot, and I thought of the night clouds gifted us electric light. I brought my car to a rolling stop and we watched the sky ignite and grant all that had been darkness a voltaic outline. We held our breath with each crack, and then I drove back to the house.

After a storm there comes a storm. And a storm and a storm. Until the night is just below 10 fahrenheit of you holding me close. The day that I arrived into the city just below the corn, the dew had been subdued and my long glance into the future had narrowed. Each blade of grass had not renewed its impertinent relationship with an axe, but each time my lips met yours, something silver - something faint - something flatware or shrapnel from the silent vectors of you wanting me so much that I felt the straw, rubyish tone of your shoulders pulling me into your timeline. You gazed at me as if my forehead had been freshly polished by the loose change in my heart's pocket. The night had not been a silver medal. The light between us was not an electroplate. While I slept like a summer storm filled with charged electricity. I did yoga - a break from Zoom - & I thought about what you asked in your moments of uncertainty, "Am I good for you? Is this love harmful? Am I suffocating you? With my problems?" One after the other like baseballs from a machine injection. I tried to think of a time when what feels natural doesn't stand between my love for you and my need for freedom. I love you with all of my heart. I love you even when stones choose to boycott noise, choose to be mute just to be mute while the river tries to make them laugh or giggle. I do yoga and I think back to the early morning hours when you were bitten blue and red by insects. Yet you tossed and turned, craving me. Craving my embrace. My body ached like the wings of a plane.

OUR SPERM COUNT IS DOWN!

We watched a magic-heist last night. It was like J.K. Rowling wrote an episode of *Law & Order* & David Mamet directed it. We thought the magicians were one step ahead of the law but the law was the greatest magician of all. We agreed the female lead was too pretty for haggard old Mark Ruffalo, who miraculously became more beautiful after shedding his false-cop persona and pulling a magical Mark Ruffalo out of his own hat. In the morning, we woke and showered together and you left your muffin in the refrigerator.

I did not leave the muffin in the refrigerator. There were two left: one for you and one for me.

In the Chancellor Hall, a reception was held. I arrived 20 minutes late & everyone asked where I got my PhD. I was ashamed to say I had only a terminal illness in fine arts.

They wore wedding bands. They talked of their husbands and wives like poison ivy something everyone must experience at least once in their lifetime. I wanted you here with me. I wanted to know what you'd think of the Chilean wine I drank from a plastic cup. And, what you'd think of the anthropologist from Puerto Rico, who said neanderthals fucked a lot and thus we inherited some of their characteristics. For instance, because we fucked a lot with them, we have a higher tolerance for plant based toxins. We also have a high tolerance for nicotine. From him, this anthropologist dressed in a light blue suit, I learned that our plant based tolerance is diminishing. We have more allergies, our sperm count is down (especially mine), and our imaginary narrative is endless, infinite. I wonder if you'd find him handsome. I learned all this when we stepped onto the outdoor terrace & took off our masks. I came back and I sat down. I wanted two plates, one for you and one to cover it. But the overly attentive waiter said, "Woman, you have two plates." I couldn't make him understand. So, I gave one plate back, but was able to get you the reception food I was allergic to: mainly food capable of sitting in the latent air too long.

I like when the car rolls over the peak to Boulder & the mountains spread open like two opaque curtains and the highway ushers me into the immensity of sky & valley & I park the car & wait & when I look up there you are! at the hood of my car, with a heavy wool sweater & two paper plates.

HANDS
TO
FACE

At the Denver airport, the line curled around the escalator, around ground transportation, the luggage carts, the baggage belts, and if it could it would curl around the Westin Hotel conveniently linked to the airport by a corridor. You had pre-check & said you'd see me on the other side &, so, I thought of death & our souls searching for each other in hell. I was hungry and, felt somewhat, demoralized. What if this line is identical to death? Is there a pre-check to make my life on earth shorter? I worry about living a long life, especially one that is filled with chronic pain. I think then my suffering will be vast and endless.

At the airport, a homeless person slept inside a sleeping bag. I thought of a hotdog - with the hotdog cozy in its interior meat. What if this human hotdog slipped out of his low-cost mechanically separated poultry soul? Where would he go and what would he do?

Yesterday, we watched a smug Brady win for the Buccaneers. We watched the young, deer-in-the-headlight Drew Lock flapping in the Broncos wind after the very poised quarterback Teddy Bridgewater was ruled out of the game for a concussion. We watched a raven - was it a raven? - bounce like a rubber ball after he caught a throw into the end zone. Here at the airport, you notice the travelers in Raven's jerseys wait in line at Southwest to return home after their team handed the first lost to the Denver Broncos. We were traitors - rooting - not even secretly - for the Ravens. Lamar stole both our hearts.

On the plane in Philly, we waited for some men in yellow vests to fix a broken panel. They looked at it, then left the plane. One returned, five minutes later, with duct tape. A woman across the aisle turned to me with wide eyes.

I turned to you, but you were typing an email to a former student and had not noticed anything. Vi, I whispered, they're fixing our plane with duct tape.

The hotel in Providence looked just like a set in a Wes Anderson film. Behind the concierge, are rows of tiny red boxes with a dangling key in each. The carpets are bright red and the floors are checkered in black and white marble. There is a glut of patterns. The elevator is old fashioned.

It is lonely and sweet to move through your past without you. Over lunch I ask whether you were always cold? Did you take the bus to New Port alone? Where did you live? You sat at a cafe, outside our window, years ago with Leslie Thorton for three hours, then walked her to the amtrak. There's the train station where you'd often wait. In the back of the restaurant, under the giant cone shaped lights, you & Eli had your first date. Michael lives near Mona's old apartment. You are moving through your history, and I sit quietly in the backseat. Outside the early east coast fall waves with green and quivering leaves. The sidewalks are made of red brick and they break around the roots of trees. You tell Michael I am a runner. It is strange for me to hear that.

In the afternoon, I sit in the fine arts museum, nervously grading papers. I expect someone to tell me I cannot be there. There's a shiny blue painting on the far wall. It looks like globs of melted sugar, dripping down its surface or foam or cracked ice. It looks like the Arctic in winter seen from the sky. I stand and cross the room to read the placard. It's called "Meltdown." It's made of oil paint, sugar, and gel wax. Upstairs, some girls laugh. It has been a long time since I sat and whispered with someone in a university building. I feel a fondness for these college girls, who laugh a little, swallow some coffee, and continue reading. In the background, the art installation videos play. When I picture you here, you are alone. You don't drink coffee. You come in from the cold and you cannot get warm, but you open your laptop and forget. You do not mind the sounds from the videos in the background. You've wrapped the remnants of some small edible thing, leftover from the night before, in plastic, and tucked it neatly in your bag. Somewhere, in the same wintery landscape, Far Wall sits in class, or takes a nap. I wonder whether Far Wall studied sitting at a desk, with a pencil in her hand, or lying down in the grass or a blanket. I wonder whether Far Wall was surrounded by a group of like-minded friends, or whether, like you, she moved through the landscape alone. Somewhere there's a writing center, and you would hurry in, your face cold and your scarf covered in snow, and Christine would wait and close the window, and you would sit down and watch her read.

Providence is lovely and lonely. It reminds me of so many other lovely and lonely places I have lived and tripped up red sidewalks, bulging over the roots of trees, spilling coffee up my sleeve.

The hotel in Providence was old and beautiful. This city you told me has amazing architecture and art. You recorded the lobby. There are mirrors everywhere. It was so cold in our room, I slept in a sweater and we curled into a ball. You were still in pain and your mind was moving like a rubber ball. There were too many places your mind had been that day, and it was still there. I ate a wonderful dumpling soup. The broth was rich and salty and green onions floated on its shimmering surface. You taught me how to cut a dumpling with chopsticks. You bought me a blueberry muffin and a coffee. We walked up the street and bought gifts for Far Wall and Miriam. I wonder whether you feel a deeper connection to these people and this history. If being here makes our love seem odd, or ill-conceived. I wonder whether in the context of so many other loves you wonder why this one. It is an odd experience, to be beside your lover's wistfulness. I wonder what kind of lover I would make in a setting that stirs up old emotions I'd thought were done with me.

In Philadelphia, under the string of lights and the canopy, I saw Calvino, sitting - so stolid - in the back row. Your posture possessed a tidiness, an elegance that is - as Marc Anthony Richardson said - bestilling. Your shoulder angled over your lap and your arm crossed your chest. Your wrist balanced on your knee. Your face in profile looked intense. I felt the agony of Calvino's longing, witness to a distance he could not cross. In his place, I would not come. I thought he is a masochist or a romantic. I watched his back recede up the sidewalk; he wore a blue collared shirt. The outline of his hair was luminous under the light, and his face was tan and almost golden. I watched him, leave and I marvelled at this: to come all the way to see you read and leave without saying hello. I touched your arm. I said, Vi. And you turned and called his name up the street. And he stopped, and my breath stilled when he looked back. Because that kind of longing makes someone hallucinate. He probably imagines you on every street and now you're really only yards away! & to turn is to compress a decade of daydreams into an instant, which is always over too quick. & so he is stolid, preparing himself to say goodbye before he's even said hello. Which is - perhaps - exactly what he's unwittingly practiced in all those daydreams and hallucinations, and so it made sense what he did next. He waved and walked on. I thought he looked sad. Because of this, I waved at him, when his car pulled up alongside our uber. You called out the open window: Calvino, how are you, and he answered, I'm breathing. Calvino, you called, and your smile was achingly beautiful, and I thought his face looked pained.

COMPLETE WITH ILLUSTRATIONS OF MAJOR CHARACTERS, SUCH AS GOD

I was so hungry, at the wine bar, I could hardly think. On my phone, I had pictures of heart valves & plastic hearts & the airbnbs where Farwall took me to recover. This was before heart surgery. The photographs. In some I am a child, shrouded by siblings, & - as you noted - looking, always intently, into an invisible distance, a different decade, maybe.

You ask how I like heist films, when I don't think anything is free. Because cost is the mystery. Because they often are a little fatalistic or end in the weightless fantasy of taking what living merits. It has, perhaps, to do with making plans, the opposite of dramatic irony, a hiccup, which the master mind, unbeknownst to us, knew would come.

This morning I woke cold and folded my torso into a sheep coat. Three months ago, in a morning just like this - I woke in your arms. My entire body tingling with electricity and desire. This morning - our bed sheets were like a sheet of ice and beneath this gelid blanket of the post-matutinal heat was

your radiating
body.

Our trip into Boulder was
short. Everything you
tried on - red, white,
or blue, or unintentionally
patriotic - made you
rubicundly sexy. Your
red skirt moved like a
matador's cape - which
could easily hide a bull.
While ironing your
serrano pepper blouse,
I studied your form as you
waited for your skirt
and blouse to stop
kissing the iron's face.

Chautauqua   Park,
crowded with dogs and
parked cars, is 14 acres of
wheat, grass, light, and
mountain. It took us
appearing clueless and confused
before we found the metal
picnic tables and benches
where Godard babysat the
taco containers. Garbo
brought a square box of
McIntosh apples. I had
been cold already, even when
you chivalrously switched
your blue hoodie with my
thin white sweater. Staring at
everyone with a mild
headache, I wish I had
brought a winter coat with me.

There were spots under the tree that were sunless and under this sunless, cotyledon defoliate-parasol, I felt cold and out of my skin. You were exquisite at conversing with students. You were natural and unawkward and I loved the way you engaged with these cool white, disaffected girls whose shyness could appear unfriendly. In my hypothermic diffidence, I studied the grass, the trash bins, the way impolite wind forced the plastic knives, the paper plates, the plastic wrappers to immigrate fast into a sea of grass, on a rudderless boat made of light and air. The wind was invasive and I felt deftly quiet and out of my skin.

I found comfort in sitting next to you: the collar of your blouse was standing straight up. There was a dog named Sesame. You told me that you put your hand in the fur of all three dogs and they were friendly. I believed you but stayed as far from them as possible. Could I easily scapegoat the invasive, abrasive wind for my antisocial proclivity at the MFA party?

In the early early evening, after our trip to the Walgreens, where you delightfully purchased an assortment of truffles, and the walk home where I used a recently purchased snow scraper to scratch your back and pull you from the path of oncoming bikers, you read me a study guide of Milton's *Paradise Lost*, complete with estimated reading times and illustrations of major characters, such as God.

In your office that afternoon, you wrapped yourself in an electric blanket.

44 was a hard year, you told me, for Milton who went blind and after his wife's death was left with 4 children, including an infant. His wife was 17 when he was 35, and they were incompatible, perhaps, due to the age difference. She went to visit her family and did not come back. In response, I think, Milton wrote pro-divorce pamphlets and argued against celibacy in marriage. A husband and wife, he thought, have a duty to replenish the earth. Eventually, she came back and died, in childbirth, shortly thereafter. Milton's house, which housed a ton of schoolboys, four babies and his wife's family, was not

conducive to his scholarship. His daughters sold some of his stuff without his knowledge. He was a Sagitarius which surprised me because he was so arrogant. Meanwhile, or before all of this Satan raped his daughter Sin and she became pregnant with Death, who eventually would also rape her, begetting Chaos. It was all so interesting. I did a wonderful job parallel parking and you told me so. We watched the Ravens beat the Chiefs, because Lamar Jackson played well. The Ravens, you said, are inconsistent. A team can't depend on one man. We watched David Mammet's *Heist.* He seems to win at the movie's end because he knew his girlfriend would betray him. Her betrayal didn't seem to faze him. He drove away smiling, though his friend, Pinky, died, and he'd pushed his lover into the hands of another man. You thought she'd fallen in love because she said, You shouldn't have sent me to him, Joe. But I thought she'd bet on the wrong man, or maybe she loved Joe and was getting back at him. There's a flatness to the women in David Mammet films, a stylized and deadpan opacity. The men in contrast are rarely not acting. Character is desire and function. In bed you whispered that sometimes you don't want to sleep. I call you Chatty Catty when you talk to me at five am until I wake. It's so long to be apart, the whole night. I lay on my back and I held your hand and

you said, let's
walk into a dream
together, Jess.

Z

LIKE ONE ENDLESS ESCALATOR TO ANOTHER ESCALATOR

In Philadelphia, lying on the very high and very white hotel bed, I received an email:

Subject: Oh no! I am dead!

If you are getting this message, you have emailed me after my death, and I am speaking to you beyond the grave. How is life back on earth?

Heaven is lovely but boring. I can fly now, but Netflix here sucks, so basically it's an even trade. Glad I got in, though--I almost didn't make it! Thank god I remembered to apologize and own up to my mistakes whenever I was wrong. That won me a lot of points! (Death Hack: you increase your chances of getting into heaven exponentially if you never tell anybody they're going to hell.) But what really cinched it was never telling a sexual assault victim it was their own fault--spoiler alert, it never is! I know because god says so.

Also, god wants you to call your mother. Call your mother!

All my love from the great beyond,

James
No email address
No phone number
Basically to talk to me you have to die first.
No need to rush, I'm up here forever
Literally
Xoxoxoxo

The reading in Philadelphia was outdoors, under a canopy strung with Christmas lights, and crowned with perfect green leaves. It was the kind of atmosphere that made me drift outside myself. It was the kind of evening that possessed a lambent timelessness. It's an epiphany that's wordless and comes at night under the stars, and you think, ok, i get it. Then it's gone and leaves a luminous sadness. Marc Anthony Richardson said if you're writing what scares you

You talked of borrowed trauma before the plane took off. I ask what you love about me

and you say my
curls.

There were many rushed footsteps,
these footfalls at the airport. I heard
them all the time as my eyes
searched for your gaze
while passengers
ascended and descended
like one endless
escalator to another
escalator moving in opposite
directions. When we landed in
Philadelphia, I remembered being
in this city before. Without you.
Your friend, Caren, was there – to
pick me up from the airport in her
hybrid Toyota. She would always
tell me if anything happened she'd
have her hybrid, but then three or
four years ago, she sold it. You are
here in this city with me. It feels
strangely familiar. With me being
born two years earlier than you.
The hotel, booked by the
university, is a large concrete
structure with a Dim Sum Chinese
restaurant tucked on the side of its
armpit. It made me think of
being in a Godard film,
perhaps his black and white
Alphaville. Except this
Alphaville has been color-
painted by modern
imagining, to re-
industrialize the cinema of
its retro-architectural
composition. We took the
elevator up and I knew even though
they offered unlimited room service
– meaning I could bill all my meals
to the room, there was to be no

room service. I felt a slight
disappointment for the both of us.

The
view
from
the
hotel on
that
10th
floor
was
expansi
ve.   In
the
mornin
g, it was
mildly
foggy as
if the sea
had
come in
to
donate
its sleep
to   the
city,
except
there
was   no
sea.

Only the skyscraper being
airbrushed   and   made

fuzzier or thin by the tip of the invisible pen of the cloud's unimpulsive penmanship.

Inside the elevator I touched your hand and I felt my love for you flood the elevator buttons and everything lit up like a Christmas that has lost all of its ornaments except for one.

We waited for Daisuke to arrive, but their bus had been delayed. I asked you to pick a restaurant for us and you chose Sampan.

I ordered pork bao, calamari papaya salad, and steak hanger for all of us. The plates of the baos arrived in a pair of two. One sat cold near a small lit candle in a short glass. They looked like two white pac-men, the marinated pork and their fat tongues, eating you as you ate it. You ate musingly, enjoying Sampan's lustrous, lambent ambience. At the table was a box of one hundred chopsticks – when Daisuke arrived in their white coat to join us, tall like a lamppost along the freeway – I took one chopstick after the other from their metal rectangular-shaped canteen and used them – one endless stream of chopsticks to serve us. Every dish seemed tasty – but the papaya salad was my favorite. Daisuke seemed to know how to order and you seemed to know how to choose an ideal restaurant for all of us.

At the hotel, you, Daisuke, and I Zoomed Far Wall, who was petting her son, Chai, in her Shreveport apartment. Provoked by me, Far Wall mentioned her inner thighs. Meanwhile Daisuke and I exchanged gifts. There were books and jackfruit chips and tiger balms and intense eye drops that could make elephants' eyeballs think they are Venus and Jupiter. Daisuke and I slept poorly. I hung my feet in the hotel's darkness while Daisuke slipped out to vacate their chronic insomnia. They were painstakingly quiet, considerate, slipping sleep into us while they were wide awake, restlessly waiting for us to wake.

In the morning, Daisuke and I began our drone filming for the Funeral project. You were sitting in bed, emailing and grading. After several failed attempts, with the drone crashing against the hotel's mirror and wall, the Tello drone took flight, floating in the air like a mechanical mosquito. We decided to name it Belial9. Nine being Daisuke's favorite number. Belial 9 gave us finite footage, some with my hair flapping against her attached camera. You were trying to get out of frame. You worried that the drone would confuse your pile of hair for a beehive and that it would stir this beehive into action and an entire colony of 1,000 bees would all come rushing out of your hair for a cinematic bedlam.

While Belial9 was recharging, we walked down Chestnut Street. We stopped by Boba King for some boba tea. We walked a long walk without knowing that we walked extensively and mindlessly. We walked the wrong way into nowhere. When we returned, we filmed you and Daisuke behind a laced curtain, converting your mouths into ghosts and terror.

Providence did not break my heart. This time around. I don't believe it ever did. Breaking my heart, that is. In this city, I do not feel lost nor lonely. My life here, was once, filled with domestic abuse, bruised plums, colored pizzas, and shifting ambitions. There were cold nights colder than an embittered ice cube, yet Providence is not my past's nemesis. It's quiet and radical and there, luring me into the sea. Not necessarily to drown me away, but to remind me that there is sagacity in proportions.

I did not know how to explain
                this
city to you. Its India Point, its quirky
        trolley
bus system, its hilly sidewalks. I watched you drink some pellegrino sparkling water under a dimmed tree in the middle of the afternoon.

We slept two nights at the Graduate like two blocks of ice. For two nights, we converted our breath under the bed sheets into steamed water. Pain continued to visit my body. At some point we sat at a bench on Thayer Street, you ate a blueberry muffin and I ate chickpeas to hold us over before our dinner at a fancy place on Hope St. 10 years ago, I did not feel any hope on Hope St. I felt God did not love me.

INTERMITTENTLY
LIKE LOUISIANA RAIN

In Salt Lake, I walked the neighborhoods on winter nights, guided by the warm blue glow of windows and tv screens, flickering on the snow. Even this cold loneliness contained the balmy promise of a someday.

NOW the flamboyant neon style of *Gunpowder Milkshake* spatters the blank walls of our unconscious minds with sequined bowling lanes and diners & even the whites of our eyes are glittery.

I love this movie!

& our someday & Michelle Yeoh - the great martial screen artist - & look at that vest & surely these are lesbians! Yes! Or are they baiting us, with a breathy death so easily mistaken for a bloody kiss? And if you want it bad enough, it is. It was a good movie. All the men were bad and the women, who killed them, seemed to like each other. It was a really good movie, we agreed. The bowling jacket, an homage, maybe.

Today's potential equity raise raised only your eyebrow. I watched you across the kitchen table as you tried to do some proprietor math. Leah has been an agent of alacrity and the university may be scared of her. I soaked mung beans in a small pot and placed our bath towel over it like Djokovic - after losing the first set and then second and eventually the last to Daniil Medvedev - placed his towel over his head. Meanwhile, we need white and green onions for the canh khoai. I also wanted to walk with you because my period is heavy and I had taken a photo of cotton or a wintery storm in the Denver light. The sun behind you and its shadows plaster themselves across your back like a Pollock.

The air is cool and you ran through the park where they were setting up a screening of *WestWorld*. The street smelled incredible when you rounded the corner and a man in the narrow alley hid a spliff behind his back and you jogged past. Two girls with enormous dogs stood in the park. Earlier, at the grocery store you bought onions, chocolate, and salt. I made pork and soup and the broth turned purple. We ate spicy tofu bites packaged individually like small candy and our lips burned. The sunlight is crisp and clean & the air never shimmers with heat. Phone wires are full of birds and nostalgia. The air smells like fresh cut grass. Now that the joyless cop show is over, what will we do with our evening and our afternoon?

We walked beyond the railroad track, under the bridge, and through the tunnel with its electric graffiti headdress. You asked about Qi. You asked if your body was open and if there was a door to your life force. We walked and walked, walking past the pile of trash which soiled the elegant and clean architecture of the RiNo Art district. We walked past The Hub, the pole dancing class, the Walnut Liquor store, and the city opened her long, athletic legs to us. There were so many pathways into the future of our nomadic exploration. When we walked back to Natural Grocers, you were holding in your arms two babies: an aluminum water bottle and the Bread and Butter Cab, which you said I loved and which you got for us when we visited Farwall in Shreveport. From across the railroad track, we could see faintly the Zeppelin Station from our peripheral view. When we took the elevator to the 4th floor of our Blueground, you were holding a box of ginger beer, ginger chocolate, one Bosc pear the color of the sepia earth before mankind ruined it with greed and capitalism.

You hated *Superman & Lois* though Tyler Hoechlin's teeth were sharp and white as a wolf's incisors and Bitsie is the name of the actor playing Lois and this appears to be her only real misfortune. One reviewer wrote: the show brings the superhero brand back down to boring earth. But I liked the premise: would superman make a good father? Though I think a daughter may have been more interesting than two teenage boys. It failed the Bechdel test by a long shot. I don't think two women spoke to each other in the pilot, though there were three women in it. You found the premise of a small town gone awry somewhat compelling. You enjoy small town conspiracies and small town America taking on the corporate world. But Lois "the greatest journalist in the world" was unbearably basic and lacked the ambition that made her a little dangerous in former iterations. She was a fearless journalist, who much to Superman's chagrin, was almost always about to get killed. One review said Superman spends too much time blinking at his family in handsome concern and darting around the stratosphere that he never can anchor his family or his show. I did not know how bored you were until we switched to *Nevers* and the deft and dapper Victorian ladies, twirling parasols and pithy phrases, roused you from your stupor.

After showering, we walked to the grocery for bacon and a gluten free muffin. The light was both lambent and radiant, coating everything we touched or saw with a sheen of translucent warmness. Denver has such clean air. If you were in Lafayette, there would be sunlight, berated by sporadic bursts of rain and lightning. The air there is thick and muggy as if the city has been hooded by a black bag, tossed, and kidnapped into a moving, get-away van. I don't like the idea of your natural oxygen tank being kidnapped by a city that only loves you intermittently like Louisiana rain. We woke unexpectedly late. Though at 6 am, my eyes were wide like long windows in a high rise office in New York. I tried to close them, but my nipples were becoming electrical poles as if a wire traveled between my cunt and nipple, and birds needing to take a break from their long flights could land on it for rest and mindless repose. Our periods have made us tired. We sleep early now. We make love less. Our pads soaking in useless iron.

Last night, you fell asleep at 9 o'clock. Tonight you've reserved a table at a winery with outdoor seats. You've been looking up galleries. We need to go to Walgreens but exhaustion overtook us. You slept while I finished blending sweet mung beans and tapioca. They do not collect the trash on Fridays or Saturdays. Though they seem to vacuum the hallways on Saturday mornings. If you look out the window long enough you'll notice the yellow fence & the ferns that burst from behind it, the gravel lot where cars park, and the broken wooden crates that rest against aluminum siding. This is a city still being built with empty lots where trash gets tangled in the weeds, gravel lots, steel beams - and on the main strip a string of new apartment complexes sit empty as old warehouses, some breweries and wineries startle the sidewalk like an old friend in an empty airport. On Friday night a live band played at the beer garden, and the train scooped lumps of people up and dumped them on the sidewalk like scoops of icecream or that Twombly painting - they shuffled up the street pushing bikes & sipping beers from cozies. I think of the castrated photographer, pushing his bike through snow to my doorstep every night, and all the gifts he gave me that I shoved into a box inside my closet. On Saturday morning, the streets are deserted. There's a slight breeze. The sunlight and the air is so clean the slight chill is crisp but not 51 degrees as our phones inform us, by 1 o'clock the city will inch its way to 90.

I ATE

A GH
OST

Because some characters had the tendency to appear suddenly, & Wol Ha died twice, & Kang Woo's mother was incestuously outraged though self-restrained upon finding her son's room stuffed with poorly executed sketches of the dead girl's hair & face you called, the k-horror/drama a comedy & though we were intrigued we did laundry & discontinued watching. The clothing kept tumbling from the machines to the floor, which gave an impression of filth due to the laundry facility's overwhelming scent of litter-box, the potency of which continually astonishes us. A puddle of dog piss glistened on the elevator floor this morning and by evening blackened into a gummy ink smudge. I thought it looked like the thumbprint of a giant or the silhouette of a racing pig. You called it Satan's thumb. We climbed into bed early. I drifted off to sleep and woke to the clacking of your computer keys.

You said even a ghost has a presence, but I don't; I pull you into a void with me. I wanted to watch the Chiefs play against the Chargers, but I couldn't find it on our CBS channel. Instead, in the background, the Chicago Bears were pummeled by the Browns who have Mayfield. And, who doesn't like Mayfield?: he's accurate and rarely throws an interception. His interception against the Kansas City Chiefs was an exception - he lost his footing and the ball landed in the arms of the 174 pound Honey Badger.

We walked to the Zeppelin Station, in the late afternoon, & met my former student, Jason. He is tall, kind, and lanky. Over his shoulder, he held a thin tote bag. The high elevation of Colorado made me continually drowsy - I tried to keep my eyes open. You spoke eloquently of Louisiana & I slept silently with my eyes unbolted by their lids. We sat on the cushioned wooden steps that lead to the upstairs bar. The setting like high school bleachers with a better view: an open garage door, a sidewalk, some food trucks, and a city street with stairs rising & rising up to

In the early morning, you reclined on the sofa, & talked to your mother. Your voice had the fluidity of champagne bubbling over the lip of a flute. I loved hearing you. You sounded so relaxed like a chill beer glass. Your ebullient echo bouncing around our high ceiling loft like a ping pong ball. Before we departed our apartment, we took out the trash. They don't collect trash here on Fridays and Saturdays, the days where denizens of a building are more likely to host parties & accumulate waste.

the glass walkway over all the moving trains. We could not find you a coca-cola, save the one displayed on the counter of a closed coffee shop. The bartender of an unrelated business sold it to us. Jason sipped a ginger beer & I got quarters. Pacman was a draw: I won the most rounds, and you ate a ghost. We played skee-ball on the broken machine until we each got our ball inside the tiny mouth of the 10,000 point ring.

The light from Denver had faded or was fading. You came in from the outside with a grocery bag full of wine & cheese & alliaceous things. Half of my eye was on the game between the 49ers and the Packers while I diced the sausage and garlic and shallot. Aaron Rodgers was throwing well. But the referees were inequitable & overzealously penalized the Packers for two silly phantom DPI calls. They ruled a 49er incomplete catch as a catch. No penalty on an egregious helmet-to-helmet contact. No call on an obvious intentional grounding. But, a backward fumble from Jimmy G - the pornstar - and poor time management from the 49ers led the Packers to win on the 49er's own turf. This is why one can't count their eggs before they hatch. The 49ers were celebrating with 37 seconds left when Rodgers threw a high ball over a pile of red jerseys. After all, he is the King of the Hail Mary. You were happy the 49ers lost because the 49ers clobbered the Bills in a Super Bowl a long time ago. 1990 to be precise. I learn from this that your rancor and aversion can last long. We ate your wonderful dish with white wine. A chardonnay. I was happy the Packers won because during the draft, Rodgers was profoundly scorned. The 49ers chose nobody Alex Smith over him. A Californian boy, he dreamt of playing for the 49ers - imagine his disappointment as he was the last person in that empty room with round tables and empty chairs, waiting for someone to want him. Once chosen by Green Bay, imagine his heartache and his embarrassment and his patience as he sat on the bench for 3 years waiting for Brett Favre to indulge in his bigotted retirement, farting between being a rascal racist and a pro-Trumper. And, then - Rodgers could hold his crown over the dominion of the professional draft fools.

I wouldn't root for the Packers if Brett Favre was still the quarterback. But Aaron Rogers, who Brett Favre mocked all through his early years, is more than enough for me to root for the team, though his teammates continue in Favres' tradition of mocking him. His sexuality is ambiguous, they say, because he never brags about his penis.

The way light refracts off roof tops is oddly reminiscent of a swimming pool. I have longed lately for my parents home in Tennessee. I imagine them old and on that terrace, looking out at the trees around the lake, somehow outside the land of those alive, and waiting for something. It saddens me. I have been thinking of how the familiar can suddenly become strange, and when and how a habit might suddenly become uninhabitable. Like the loneliness of my bed in Lafayette, where I learned one Wednesday morning of my brother's death. Of late, dread infuses the idea of returning to it. In that Abrons story, she spoke of the face of the sky, falling. Some morning in the rain soaked streets. Some pleasant evening, when, in the East Village, he ushered me into a cab. Sitting at a dinner table one Thanksgiving in Salt Lake, waiting for my brother, who was so late, to arrive from Las Vegas, with the broken cherry pie he baked. *Who,* he said, *will be thankful for this?*

IS YOUR MIND A FLY OR A REPTILE?

This morning churned toward us damply like the door to a dryer opened prematurely and the day - a tangle of wet clothes - tumbled into the tops of our heads and coated our brains in a gummy dampness. In a dream my forehead was wet like condensation on a beer glass; sweat rolled off my nose & I sopped it up with a dusty rag and when the rag grew wet, I wrung it out. I looked like someone else, but I was late for *my* interview. In the morning, I learned that you'd been cold all night - though your skin was a furnace against mine, your body was a block of ice.

Sometimes I wonder whether your mind moves like a fly or a reptile, and if a reptile then what kind? We spend so much time trying to adjust the temperatures of our bodies. How do you define sentimentality and do you like it? Esther Perel says love is not a permanent state of enthusiasm. Do you think that's too obvious?

In an interview once, I mentioned an amphibian. I think my mind can walk on land, but has a vast oxygen tank for water and algae. So, if my mind is the tail of a salamander, it probably can endure any kind of fire. Sentimentality is the hedonistic preservation of something that should have died. I don't think Perel encourages things that stay stagnant. Thus, her sentiment for enthusiasm is short-lived.

Drowsiness continues to dominate my Monday. I drift in and out of sleep and tiredness. My head feels heavy - like two hundred tons of buffalo hide pressing my awareness down. My eyelids feel heavy. I had no choice but to climb into bed. After a Zoom conference with a student, you climbed in with me. You asked about my experience in refugee camps. My father had it worse. The Viet Cong put him in a cage the size of a chicken coop, fed him polluted water & spinach in a semi-flat metal bowl, and he suffered from starvation and dehydration. At one point, his penis expelled a stone and it bounced against the dirt floor like a marble ball. In your arms, I told you, I left most of my life behind last year. There are only remnants of me here. Most of me left this world a long time ago. When you went to pee, I began a phone call with Anthem Health care while baking tofu on wax paper. I sauteed cabbage, which you love. And, I made red sauce for the days when we are famished on time. You were hungry so you snacked on cheese and almond crackers.

It's Monday night so the Eagles are playing against the Cowboys. What more can I say: I dislike both teams. Prescott, I like, but the cowboy's silver and blue uniforms will always strike me as smug.

In the evenings, the light glows on the stringed bulbs along the backs of fences and sheds. We passed an alley where reeds overran the rusted train tracks and weeds cropped up against the sides of rickety buildings with aluminum sides. Sometimes the doors have elaborate metal grates that look gothic and ornate. In gravel alleys, green crops up and sprouts in long stalks. The road is empty, and in the distance a train clatters, and when we round the corner, people laugh and drink wine off glass tops of repurposed barrels. Zeppelin Station has two metal doors painted red & they're reminiscent of the bunkers in apocalyptic films. We played free skee-ball, and you danced a frantic Charleston, and I laughed so hard I nearly choked. I cashed in a dollar for a game of pac-man, which you won, though I ate the most. In the evening, on the rooftop, we discovered a billiard table. The clink of billiard balls echoed out into the sky. The bright yellow lights and the train, clattering. Someone on a balcony below lit a cigar and the blue smoke drifted up. It was dark and we could barely see the balls.

We'd watched *I Will Destroy You.* And in the elevator you asked what I like about it. I like how survival and laughter coexist. How the impact of trauma goes quietly unnoticed. How the characters try to avoid it. It's too real to watch too long. I like your definition of sentimentality. My brother, John, once told me it's for people with no real sentiments. At the time, I really liked that, but it was a quote from someone else. I can't remember who. Ironically, sentimentality may be the emotional equivalent of quoting someone else. But I forgive John for that: It was, afterall, an affirmation he gave me long ago, when we were not yet 20, sprawled on a rug, passing a spliff, and trying on ideas we had not lived.

You were cold in the morning and I was sorry for not turning up the heat. You'd slip out into another frigid morning and spend all day trying to get warm again. There was something in your posture, which suggested you wanted something from me. But I was drying off and did not know what it was. I said I'd pick you up in the evening, and when you left

I remembered the man who spoke to you on the platform and wondered whether I should have gone with you to the station. And that nagging feeling followed me into the day and sat, warm, inside me, like a pot of coffee.

It was dark when I kissed your early morning lips. In the dark, they looked like barbecued green beans. I was hoping to climb out of bed before the alarm clock disquieted us both into matutinal submission. I spent nearly half an hour in the shower with the hot water riding on my back while I tried to get warm. When you peeled the shower curtain apart to greet me, I jumped slightly. Your face appeared like a butler had placed your head on a plate. I turned my head & searched for the remaining content of your body, but the curtain swung its fabric door closed before my eyes could make their deft progression.

When I walked to the train station, I kept praying that

the elevator would work. Climbing three flights of stairs wasn't something my morning heart was ready for. My afternoon body was something else entirely. It spent the rest of the day in a half-gelid, half-hypothermic state. My feet are prune-cold. I wanted to climb into someone's pizza oven and sleep. While eating white rice, I wondered what your students thought of Abrons' "Context." If they liked her bucket of rain water.

My posture was that of an old crone - tired of the cold, tired of existence, tired of everything. I wanted nothing from you but your warmth. Or your furnace. You extended your inferno, but left the oven by the side of the road where mice climbed in and out of an eye socket like a pothole. My students from both my fiction and poetry class greeted me warmly. I pondered the source of their warmth. They were often - behaving like they were too cool to be in my class. Too white to learn anything from me. But today, there was verve in their voices. Their young throats held two coffee mugs of enthusiasm.

Before falling asleep last night, I was dressed from top to bottom in long sleeves and flannel pants. Even though my body exuded heat, I was trembling like a leaf in the wind. And, you didn't like one-sided vulnerability so you climbed out of bed and added a shirt to your soul. I confess now I didn't have any energy to go into battle and combat with you on the dividends of sultriness or how cold our home has become. My eyelids were heavy and my mind was an elephant whose only tusk has

been sawed off by the
medium blade of
dismal thoughts.

MEN TALKING LIKE A PARODY OF MEN TALKING

I slept, while the world closed its afternoon eyes & in the sonic periphery I heard your fingertips tapping sound into technology. It faded and returned and faded and I slept many lunar moons away. I woke eventually to decline a student's request for a generous extension on a generous extension. You drifted into sleep after watching another episode of *The Nevers*. The TV show is filled with brutality, with men mistreating women like it was Salem all over again. Despite enjoying the show's clever and intelligent dialogue, it was hard for me to watch and continue watching. You don't seem to struggle with brutality on screen.

I could not watch *Ride or Die* because of the bruises on that woman's body and the murder-sex with the surgical knife. Her body littered with ecchymosis and contusion and blue and black marks, reminded me of the sky before a large storm.

Our date at Bigsby's Folly-Craft Winery was delightful. I pointed out the broken elevator and the crowd who had to ascend the stairs quickly to catch the train. I had gluten free pizza for the very first time in a very long time. We both were craving crusted flat bread. I had on a gray sweater for the occasion with stenciled words written in white, "I love you but I love pizza more."

Dark clouds hovered over the outdoor terrace. If it rained, I wondered where we'd run for cover. I watched a tall, extremely anorexic Asian cross her long legs and the young Indian man sip his wine across from her. He turned his light gray cap around and served her cheese and olives. But, she hardly ate anything. There were others at a near table - a couple with their parents. They ordered a plate of cheese with cured meat and a high population of wine glasses cluttered their small circular table. When we walked home, the sky seemed bruised like the actress whose husband used her body as a boxing bag.

I continued to bleed and my blood was thick and dark and pasty like chocolate. You described my period as those guests who – at the end of a party - linger in the doorway but won't leave. You described your period as a New York subway.

We watched *Wrath of Man*, a Guy Richie heist film. Mostly men talked and the men talked like a parody of men talking. I turned to you and asked "Is this how men talk?" There were two women. One of whom called the guys in the locker room "ladies," which shows she can traffic in the masculine though it contrasts sharply with laconic H, the film's real man.

We'd walked along 38th street, and in the distance, there were lights and tents & tangles of bikes chained to trees and parking meters. Lyft scooters were left in heaps on corners and side streets. The crowd got thick as we approached the underpass and train station. Two men pressed so close to us I felt their voices brush the top of my head. I worried they'd trample our heels and ankles. One said, "Ladies," and asked how we felt about scooters. You said you did not feel much about it. You turned your head and noticed the man in the red cap had wild eyes. The thin guy, with a red beard, and a wide brimmed hat, seemed benign. You turned back. "Have you seen," the benign - but superfluous - one asked, "the ad where old ladies kick over all the scooters?" We did not answer. "Maybe those ladies are you," the wild one said. The one with the wide-brim must've disapproved. He whispered, "Woah, dude," and peeled away from us. I grabbed your hand and walked fast. Near the tents and flashing lights, guards were checking vaccination documents. We had not brought our wallets, so we turned around, and walked the circumference of the festival. "We live in a great place," you said. If you stand on a bench on the sidewalk you can see a concert over the low wire fence. A woman, with a flannel tied around her waist, was doing this. She sang along to all of the songs. Up the block, there was another concert. Everyone seemed so young to us. On our walk home, we watched scooters zip in and out of the street. A girl almost crashed into her friends, and everyone on the block, including her, burst into laughter.

WHEN MY BODY WAS A GLASS TERRARI UM

The showerhead at 6AM lulls the blue room back to sleep. I rolled over at 6:15 and watched you wrap a towel around your head and you said good morning in your rough and sultry morning voice. In the breaks between the blinds I saw the night hang the damp & dusty clouds atop a block of square shaped lofts.

Back when I feared flying, I'd pretend airplanes were giant sleighs, rushing, rushing over the endless expanse of arctic snow.

It took longer on the drive to Boulder for the crisp outline of mountains to come into focus. Your voice was soft and distant and you read *Craft in the Real World* aloud until we grew bored of it. You wore a dark blue wrap-around dress with bell shaped sleeves and flower print. You wore a special skin-toned bra to cover up the scar bisecting your chest. At our apartment, I folded you like the stem of a flower onto the bed. Your neck smelled salty & floral. You rested your left hand between your shoulder and right breast & caught your breath. You did this the first night we lay together in a bed and my body turned to you without moving.

My travel time home from Boulder back to Denver has greatly diminished, in hardship, now that you drive to campus and collect me. Thanks to your tenderness, my teaching days are no longer as long nor as oxygen-deprived. Teaching behind a mask is a little dangerous. Even my student, Sam, stops breathing when reading out loud. I woke early for an interview, and oval spots of light traveled up and down my face like a diurnal flashlight. My face burst with luminosity like bubble wrap. Most Fridays, you are busy with Zoom meetings. Your voice echoes in our loft-ish abode like a gramophone. You are serious and friendly and I fantasize; I'd like to do something sultry and scandalous behind your laptop to make you smile. The thawed out frozen pork I sauteed in red sauce and salt had a hemoglobin aftertaste, and even the cabbage contained the iron relics of something murdered. There was nothing natural about the palette transaction.

Last night, my body hung like a glass terrarium; I felt the soil of your fingers beneath me, & the water of my orgasm floating in between each breath. Everything in me was suspended - between the elevation of your tenderness and the day's vast longing.

Your office air was cool and came through the open window. We applied for jobs in a glass building two stories up from the world and ate lunch outside and I was tired and weary of the college boys - who barked like guard dogs at the girls in sunglasses & bikini tops. When we walked across the green campus lawn & under the canopy of yellow leaves, I watched your profile against the lush trees, & students crowding the corners of the bright afternoon, feeding their hangovers with angus beef & grease, and I asked what you did for fun in college and you said you read poetry in your room. And now in your office you tell me you'd like to go back to school, in Switzerland.

Even though I took only one sip of the Bread

and Butter wine you bought, I woke feeling as if I had a hangover. We fought intensely last night with me saying many fucks. In the middle of the fight, you climbed out of bed. I could hear you in the darkness, putting on a t-shirt and pants. I could hear the sonic, crisp audio of you throwing things randomly and mindlessly into a bag and I could hear the teeth of the zipper grinding each other's molars as you zipped one bag up and began another. I suspected that you were preparing for a night stay at some random hotel. My heart quickened and I felt defeated. I began to prepare myself, my mind mainly, for a desolate night, my first night in Denver, alone without you. I thought how quickly it escalated - one moment you were in my arms and the next, you were like a young soldier who had just joined the military, sitting on the edge of the bed, waiting to say his farewell and I was that pregnant wife with a three month fetus in my womb, wondering when you would return. The argument appeared surreal as a squid fight in the rain with sharp steak knives.

But your face and chest were blue in the glowing moon and your tone softened to the tone I love and know and so I did not want to go.

The dark clouds of our bodies took a sharp turn. Sunlight began filtering through and we fell asleep into a quiet, resignated embrace.

In the afternoon, we walked to the Corner for shrimp

bowls. We waited and waited for our food to arrive. In the car ride back to Denver, I read you notes on *Paradise Lost*. Belial, the lusty fallen angel, preferred to exist than to not. He said if they (the fallen angels, including Satan) irritate God too much, he might obliterate them. The most egregious thing they could do (revenge-wise) was to "disturb" and "alarm" GOD, but otherwise, God is God. Belial suggested that "familiarity with the horror and darkness would lessen the pain of Hell." You drifted us out of the mountain sky, with the sunlight behind us, and I was thinking, Belial is so naive. Satan's daughter, Sin, was born out of his head precocial - meaning full grown. And, he raped her. And, when he raped her, she gave birth to Death, their son. And, their son, Death, inspired by his father's genetic gene pool of rape, raped his mother, Sin. Back then, you said, people didn't know how to fuck. There were limited orifices. And, they only knew how to rape. Mary was a victim of such. It was a huge inconvenience for her, you said. And, I laughed as you pulled us into the front parking lot of Blueground. Later, you read a boring flash fiction from a boring flash fiction book, and I learned you love to eat muffins and drink coffee in the parking lot of expensive pharmacies while I pack books & ship them back to 11:11 Press.

GINGER
& ANTICIPATORY GRIEF

The air was brisk when I descended the elevator into the street. A thousand tons of darkness piled on my swollen body & no light peaked through the lamps or windows. The train arrived seconds before I did. At Union Square, rain drizzled on my phone, and the screen sparked like disco lights in an empty bar.

When you sat with your back against mine, your body felt like my eyelid and I was a facemask. A pocket of steam. Your body was a pocket of steam on my eyelid. I spent the last two days in pain. Chest pain. Leg pain. You hung my legs like bats. But I didn't want my body to echolocate like those chiropteran behemoth ruins in any diurnal afternoon. I read an article about a man being bitten by a bat. He refused to get a vaccine and subsequently died of rabies a few days later.

You read a story about a vending machine that sold condoms, cunts, and sex for 5 minutes. The men in attendance wore bushy mustaches and tinted aviator glasses. They looked like undercover police. You'd meticulously plotted out the logistics. The bots zoom bombed everyone that night, but when you read, they listened. Stolid & unflappable, you dedicated the piece to robots. The wind was heavy on our walk to the grocery and the clouds were stacked like vaporized sardines. You said the air smelled incredible: like garbage, exhaust, and marijuana. I ran in the evening and when I came back you were standing, radiantly, at the vanity in your black and pink pajama top with a safety pin fastened at the opening. Vi, I said, what do you love about me? There was a moment when you kissed me in the night and I was coming freshly from a dream to meet you in the darkness. For an instant, you wore my brother's face then came into focus and I kissed your mouth. In the crisp, grey day, I ran to the station and up the stairs and over the elevated glass walkway and down the stairs and I did not stop until I came to a crosswalk and there I stood panting. The wind that rocked the red crane seemed profoundly melancholy and the stacks of thick grey clouds seemed to meld like Twombly globs and drizzle jaggedly down a tap-water canvas--I mean, the sky--that Mariam Makeba song my brother loved was rattling in my ears and I wondered if he could, would he miss it--a drumbeat, profound melancholy, anything? That's when the light changed and I ran under the bridge, where the remnants of a homeless man's tent lay like a crumpled umbrella and whose red & pink spray-painted walls had been freshly erased in a coat of grey and onto the bus stop littered with empty cups and I jogged between the cars that idled at a traffic light and down the gravelly block to our glass door, which was locked. So, I stopped.

A ROMAN EMPIRE IN SANDALS

In the morning when I left you to let darkness clothe your consciousness with the clover expansion that is often seen as light, I walk in the dark as your day takes form. There is this moment in time when I take the elevator to the train station, you realize you cannot be the sole dream analysis of my night or the figure in the dark with me. After all, in that dream Redford appeared and he spoke my legal name and it brought me great shame and embarrassment. In the same way when students address me in my legal name, I feel as if I have somehow been violated.

You spent the day coaching Whitman and Dickinson to many faceless screens. I stood before my students like a Roman empire in sandals. My fall is that I don't know what subjectivity is. And, that my students loved Langston Hughes too much. His dream deferred. His barren raisin in the sun. At night after a long bus ride and my bladder about to burst at Union Square, I wait on the platform for your small frame to come into view. I texted you about the sausage you prepped with mushrooms and garlic and tomatoes. But, the music of your phone was resiliently silent and with it the empty space expanded before my gaze. I wonder if you could see the bold, calligraphic stroke of my existence 100 meters away? My citation has been about waiting for the emergence of your body, planting unreasonable kisses on places that have been deprived by daylight.

Has your love for me been implicit or explicit? These were the words I borrowed from your Friday's consultation with another academic and the student you were advising. The meal you prepared had fermentation. It had thin square cheese that made me think of crackers. It had both us as longanimous audience for the pot's iridescent evaporation. You hovered over the stove like a spacecraft. And, I languished in my hunger waiting patiently for your love to unravel on a plate. When I poured white wine into the narrow waist of the short whiskey glass, I thought of how soft your lips are. How creamy and buttery they are as if your lips were margarine melting in the oven of my baguetted face, the left cheek of my sourdough.

On Saturday, in the morning's cool blue lassitude, we walked along abandoned sidewalks in search of coffee. We stopped at a park with wooden chairs facing west. My lungs like parched gold wheat stalks held the dry blue breeze and the green trees and pink circles painted on the sides of breweries helped me to forget my stuttering heartbeat.

Two years had passed since I climbed the stairs to a hotel bed, my body disintegrating with each step. Inside the room, where everything was packaged in a whiteness that was crisp and anonymous, I folded up my blouse and dress, tucked away my comb and toothbrush. And to make it quick and easy for my family or whoever found me, I wheeled my black luggage into the unobtrusive armpit of a hotel room and I laid my body on the bed and I waited with the fervor of a bride but did not die.

New York City glittered like a Christmas tree that winter I believed death would gift me my mollified pain in white paper and twine. Hours went by. I laid my body on the bed. I waited and death never came. My heart rate returned to seventy, and I knew I would not die that day but face twelve students and a University that paid so poorly, dying looked like an opportunity. So I did not go back to Columbia University. The following day, I flew to Iowa City and Airbnb'd my heart to a surgery. It should not take death to realize work will work you and watch you die, which is why it was unbearable to watch you that afternoon, when the wave of exhaustion licking the heals of my heart caught up, and I collapsed and watched, from the sofa,

159

while a job that pays you poorly
swallowed up another Saturday.

MANGOS LACK MOST MEANS OF SELF EXPRESSION

This morning, your voice is fog and fur floating over the city's furniture. Cranes bend their necks to kiss the ribbed rooftops. I do not think you've touched me yet. Your face is still and your lips are set. Your eyes, downcast. Your skin is the window of a cold car on a warm night. An overheated engine with a damp forehead that calls itself an ice box with no plums. Last night, your legs fell asleep like a pile of cats and I zip your arms around my neck and carry your body to the toilet.

From our RiNo window on Wynkoop, I drank coffee and glanced down
at the parking lot. The sun appeared unapologetic, casting its shafts of light on the car's gleaming bald heads. Here Subarus are high in population. In a city not too far from here, the headquarters of Blue Moon.

Beer isn't a to-go beverage of mine, but with the way the heat coruscated along the sides of the industrial silos, it seemed that the sun was sipping beer all the time, making everything in its vicinity sweat with a quiet, contemptible disdain. The kind a teenage boy would give his parents for skateboarding in the middle of the afternoon without a hat on, where the heat is high.

with a series of feverish kisses we had christened our new modern abode by midmorning, we clung to each other on our immaculate white sheets like octopus tentacles to the sea floor. Our pillows were like the Pope's paws, holding our heads in place like a religion. When Blueground asked us to rate our check-in, we did not hesitate to tell them it was great. With exception to the missing smoke alarm and a broken vanity drawer and although it seemed like a bear had chewed on the corner of the bed platform, everything appeared hospital to us. I slept a full night of sleep - meaning I slept well.

But, you, housing water in your body, slept quite poorly. The salt content of the bacon we ate had a way of leaking its piquancy into you. Blood stream and all. I thought you didn't notice when I lingered nakedly near the bathroom floor, waiting for your lustful gaze to fall on me. I discovered later my body isn't an ideal place to deny you intimacy. You did notice, but your body was too inflated like a waterbed to be erotically present.

I had to find a way to stop the engine of your imagination from transporting itself like twitchy cargo from one end of the city to the next.

In your arms hours later, I learned that you very much desire and crave to make love to me in the early morning hours of our waking. Out of your skin and with the light falling intermittently on your nipples, I tell you that I am like a full glass of water, filling to the brim with unfiltered happiness. I love this city. It's so poise.

There is clarity here. It's a city where squared light like sheets of polychromatic origami paper behave like diurnal disco lights on your nude form. When the train quietly rolled by, one leg marching over the other like soldiers during the Civil War, I tell you to love me with your hands, your hips. Let us explore the city together, I whispered into your high cheekbone. Let us not rinse our orgasms away because this city is so dry.

By mid-afternoon, I am in your arms again. You were resting on the sofa and I crawled into you and asked you, unprovoked, do you think bisexuality is confusing? Last night we took the train to Union Station where the streets are full of tables and children run through the water fountains. In Boulder most buildings have jagged peaks to emulate the mountains. From our window, Denver is a city of scaffolds and box trains. The giant murals are bright blues and yellows and pinks. The sunset burns your silhouette into a wall. Your back is curved and fades into the thick slatted shadows of our blinds.

At Union Station we were dumbfounded by the newness of

our new lives. We spent an hour walking around the biggest wholefoods I have ever been inside. Then you gingerly selected two ripe avocados and five ears of corn to buy. Is it strange to see telephone poles lining city streets? You did not know which train to take. We had no tickets and no one noticed. You looked anxious with your chin raised, and your eyes darting around the train.

I wanted to buy you icecream but the meat in my backpack would grow warm. So we went home and we ate mango cheeks, a distinction you found strange considering mangos lacked all other means of self expression. Is it violent, I wondered, to give and take away a mango's face? From the window, over your shoulder, I see a train glide slowly behind a green building with a grey peaked rooftop. We have taken to waking at 6AM and falling asleep at 10:30. There are so many ways to fill a single day.

By evening I had already filled the corn squash with

165

kale, pork sausage, rosemary, and yellow onion. I have been wanting to open the new chapter into our home with this signature dish of mine. Our rice cooker has been huffing and puffing like a fat pig. But tonight, everything changes. The way mountain light falls first on your face before washing over mine.

I plated the table - a pair of forks, two glasses of water, short glasses for wine. Even furnished, the tall wine glasses are so fragile. It reminds me of your stomach: so easily crumpled. But, I broiled everything for you. I didn't pull the pork from the refrigerator until I had to. Sitting in the sausage pan, the onions and kale and sausage must have gotten to know each other so well by now. Even when we sat together on the sofa, my body leaning into yours like one plate onto another in a china cabinet, and watched *Manifest* manifesting its Death Dates, its metallic, iridescent peafowl onto our TV screen - I felt God had stopped by and window washed my soul. It's now lucent and less opaque. When I smeared chocolate on it - the view into my radiant existence was still penetrable.

At night, I slept and spoke to you in my sleep. It's some gibberish, slightly paraphrased brief monologue. It's impossible for me to brush my teeth now. I always feel the urge to expose my pubic hair to the vanity sink which is mirrorless from my hip down; I must take precautions. I hid behind the dresser and when you emerged tepidly into the dim hallway, I waited. I'd waited with my ear against the wall and heard the engine in your electric toothbrush revving. You took to brushing your teeth there for fear the vanity sink would have the same inexplicable effect on you, would inspire the same seductive calling in your hips to be freed of your elastic waist bands.

Living with a lover, the weekends feel like real holidays, to wile away the day in another's company, the sound of steel pots welcoming their steamy lids behind me, reminds me of that time you said my hand on your left breast feels like a plastic lid latching onto the lip of a paper coffee cup; it fits.

So often we watch tv like this, and fall asleep like this. You laugh into your laptop or a steaming pot, and your joy is solitary as a child's. We both especially laugh when our Kind sponge expands to three times its normal size. I watch you hover over the soup pot while I read my student's synopsis. The aroma of pork ribs and the onion lend themselves a particular kind of slanted truth that permeates in the domestic undertone. In the morning, I sunk through the fluff of a comforter and you pulled the white sheets between us and kept them there, though you had sat up, squinting into the sunlight so long ago.

Last night, you showed me drone shots of a dead love in a dead valley. Then closed the laptop quickly to save the tender exuberance of the past from the shock of knowing we'd snuck up on it. And so, I too, shut my eyes, like the door to an occupied bathroom stall I'd mistaken for vacant. I lean over and press my mouth to your eyelid. You keep typing.

You are everywhere you've been and here.

Our apartment is cold and colder now. With the air conditioner working so well, I feel like a full chicken being chilled on the counter top. **The extremity parts of me turn light purple.** We had a full day yesterday, accomplishing so much in a very short time. **We woke up early** - like 5 or 6 am early, **even before the sun showed her golden mango face.** I finished another recommendation. You collaborated with Sarah from Montreal and wrote in Norwegian with Miriam from Geirangerfjorden. Waking up early expands the consciousness of our day. We even had time to watch three episodes of *Manifest*. We are at the scene where **death is fervently knocking on Zeke's door: he is slowly freezing to death. His ears are bruised purple and his fingers, toes, and legs severely freezer burnt.**

When we descended the elevator to the laundry room - where our detergent has to be a high efficiency thing as well- we felt as if we had shifted into a world where poison behaves like a bicycle rack four floors below us. In your arms, I watched Toshio

Matsumoto's *Funeral Parade of Roses*. It's your assignment from a zealous artist living in Brooklyn. Not too far from where I once lived. It took us a while to navigate through the Criterion Channel and if the password was the beast must be killed or the beast must die, but I was able to troubleshoot it for you. In our studio apartment, the black and white cinematic texture laced our gleeful faces with a kind of textual chorus that often exists in drive-in movie theaters. I have been dreaming of taking you to one. I think it's deeply romantic. Japanese transgender culture from the late 1960s seemed to be full of carnations and violence that moves like calligraphical strokes. We were so in awe of Matsumoto's showerheads and the landscape of men's nipples which behaved more closely to a standing lamp's foot switch than to the nipples of mammals.

You were full of sleep during our viewing of it, but I was too engrossed in it to notice. Our afternoon languished away and later, after a short run in our RiNo neighborhood, where I was heaving heavily from the high elevation of Denver's metropolitan climate, I showered and reclined on our long sofa. I coughed and coughed like I smoked two cartons of Marlboro cigarettes. I could run in

Lafayette for twenty minutes, but a five minute run here feels like an unbearable full hour.

Meanwhile you carried yourself like a flower that's dead. At night you hung your legs. I pressed them to your chest. I rested my chin in the arch of your foot. Your heart beat like a daisy. *A blooming. The same sound waves play. Like circumambulation.* What can I do, I asked. Nothing, you said. I can't tell the difference between your fatalism and confidence.

Later, in the cool blue light, I walked you to the bus stop. We paused on the overpass to take photographs of a train huffing fat grey clouds over the rusted tracks. You were pleased you wore the black tights under your dress. *Jess,* you said, *let me ask you a question.* Maybe a nightmare is not your mind turning on itself, I thought. Maybe, only in a dream, you are safe enough to feel afraid. *Jess,* you said, *I have a question.* I waved and the train clattered away.

My tongue was lugubrious in the afternoon. Fat and drunk, my tongue passed out in the hallway of my mouth. All afternoon, the words tripped over it on their way out. I mentioned my brother in my fiction class. My realization dawned slow as condensation in a glass. Hours later on the white concrete, in a sun so bright, *I'm sad!* I thought and squinted my eyes.

Didion can't give me my dead brother's wisdom, though I still need it and can't find it. He loved *Slouching Toward Bethlehem* best. From Louisiana to Arkansas, I listened. On the way to his funeral, there was a sign for Jamestown and a sign for Williamsburg. I laughed. I said *Jesus Christ.* I said *I get it.* I drove into a hailstorm. A fourteen wheeler nearly blew my car over. I whispered *be with me.* I sobbed into the steering wheel. While filling a prescription for lexapro, I sobbed. Then laughed out loud because it was the kind of joke he loved. Back then I laughed a lot. I thought it is a cosmic joke, life, what I know, and I thought *he is with me* and I thought *we are laughing.* Now I wonder whether I'll spend my life listening to Didion. Though, I suspect, he'd have grown out of it and given me a different book. Or his relationship to it would mature into nostalgic attachment. And now my love will be like that. As if I have adopted his nostalgia and I am raising it myself.

And then, I felt like I'd been dropped inside a bottomless bag of sand, and so sure that I would never find my way out again, I wondered Vi, have you ever been so bored by a dream you willed yourself awake again and that heavy sand that burned my lungs and stomach vanished. I could have whistled all the way home, with your light grey bag of frozen shrimp, garlic, chardonnay, butter and milk chocolate. Sometimes all it takes is a bag of groceries to transport my body into the weightlessness of futurity, like lifting oneself over the lip of a swimming pool, and the heaviness that was not yours, drips off. The passage of time can feel like this: like committing a crime and getting away with it. That must've been what Robert Frost meant. I could have whistled and skipped all the way back to our apartment.

In the afternoon, I read an interview in *Bomb. You're really involved with interviewing people,* I read, and Calvino was the interviewer. I remembered the clip of cyprus trees dancing in a hurricane, their ghastly halos of blue rain. *I think I am everything.* You said. Dear God, I am God, I thought. *I've always been the person I've always been,* you said. I thought, I love you. I thought, don't die. I thought, tonight, we will eat garlic shrimp and milk chocolate. I was deep asleep when you woke up from insomnia. You tossed and turned like you knew how to tango horizontally, but with my heavy lids and slow moving mouth, I inhaled the early morning light and fell into the back of the morning. My back riding with the backs of dark shadows as they climbed in and out of window sills. Shafts of light have a way of traveling by staying still. You woke up from a dream. You whispered your dream into my faintly fading ears. In the quiet distance of the morning, I heard, "The wind was so

abrasive and you were there."
Yesterday, after a long day on campus, you came home to me.

MEANWHILE MY HEART TWIRLS LIKE A DRUNKEN DAISY

Listen, our rice cooker is having a cesarean delivery. Eventually, we'll devour its babies and wonder at the kinship between last night's fever dreams and breakfast this morning.

The warm sweaters and underwear in our canvas sack are sylvan and slick; we go on existing.

A sunset is not happiness, though our pillows are white and plush and soft as angel cake. On the floor beside a discarded sock there's a table with a round, wood top. So, we can put our feet up.

In bed, our temples nearly touch. You can't stand the idea of never seeing anyone you love again and so go on existing.

Meanwhile my heart twirls like a drunken daisy, and it frightens you. Because a heart should not really bloom.

Take this head of lettuce, which meant to live, and look what came of it? Take Lispector! She wished to exist forever, as long as her body would let her. She lived long, masticated in the denouement of Pernambuco's great yawn. Time is a mouth of many teeth, darling. You think art is a deck of tarot cards. You pull the high priestess from the oceanic bedsheet, but you don't really believe it.

Then you come shoeless, scatter the gulls, fling clumps of wet sand at my blanket and I cup my hand to my brow but the sun comes so insistent- as if it never considered an alternative - I might be a beach house battered by a cyclone. Light pries the splintered wood apart and stings my eyes. You hold a conch shell to the sky and saltwater drips onto my cracked lips. You don't get it. There are more ways than one to end thirst.

Now that we live near the mountains, you wander away from your intelligence and like Whitman go bathe and admire yourself. Still you like to exist. What if your image of death was this: your head against my chest, my song bringing you to rest, then maybe you'd feel different? Remember the song you called strange with words you could not understand. The song I was taught in school.

When I was seven, maybe six, I sang on the red road home from school, I sang to a naked woman, with her bush of pubic hair, clinging to a cold wall, and when she wore misshapen slacks, the men followed and taunted her and offered her old bills to take them off. Her mind was not right but I saw shame in the angle of her bent head. The house flooded. Water brought pig intestines into our rooms and trash clung to brick floors. My mother sewed all day and into the night. She could not stop to eat.

These images have burnt holes into my mind. You don't get it. You get what CD Wright once called my self-protective innocence. And you marvel at the insight. I sang a song you could not understand but you felt I'd bailed it from a well so deep the opalescent water grew tar-thick and black as pitch and your ragged breath grew steady and

you   fell   asleep
against my chest.

THE DAY UNFOLDING LIKE A TRASH BAG

I saw you from our 4th floor RiNo window. A black ink blot, nodding across the periphery of my memory. I think it was your gait, so dogged and exhaustion-hobbled. I was in our sofa's beige embrace, when the sky's cool blue lassitude drew me to the window. You descended the stairs of the platform and vanished briefly from my gaze. I watched until the steel doors blinked you away.

At our kitchen counter, I had been busy cutting the heads of a mini broccoli tree which I could hold in my palm like a child. I brought butter which later went well with the oaky taste of the 2017 Chardonnay. I have been so romantic, waiting like a wife to prepare our home a meal that is transcendent as the way the empyrean sky of Denver unsaturated its thick margarine of de-illuminated light. You asked me to come meet you halfway between the train station and our apartment. I hop down the elevator. And, with a mask on my hand, I walked to you.

My feet feel light, lighter than a pencil mark on a piece of paper. You smiled enervatedly when my gaze met yours. I tossed your backpack over my shoulder and we walked home like two lamp posts. Though the way you walked, it seemed as if you had returned from a war - not Iraq nor Afghanistan nor Vietnam, but closer to the Civil War when Abraham Lincoln was the President. And, I greeted you like a war nurse, searching your fatigued face for bruises, lesions, impairment, incapacity. You returned from the war of existing - in high elevation Boulder - like a wounded soldier.

You told me - the day unfolded like a trash bag - where someone - life probably - threw you into a black sack and tied its top in a tight knot. Inside, you fought the inevitable suffocation with your sluggish fists. But no one came to untie you. Left you there while you diminished, suffocated, camouflaged out of existence. I came rushing immediately to you - to witness the lassitude of your immense desire to see me converting into mutual excitement - to draw our defocused bodies into full view.

It's not true what happened between us - the time between you leaving for work and the time of you arriving home. It's not true what the side view mirror says: that the objects are closer than they appear. As you walk toward me with open arms, you are closer to me because you are closer. We walked and walked until we reached the huge silos of our neighborhood building structure. When I walked you to the station early this morning, there were squared lights that illuminated a reticent, vacant city inside of them.

I tried to squeeze too much into one day. Poe and his heart heart tale should unravel in a week, but I wedged it all into one small afternoon. You had an image of me stuffing two pounds of cranberries in a small turkey: its monarch butterflied stomach overstretched, inflated like a child eating two loaves of stone after starving for three months straight. You did not tell me this, but your heart was twirling like a drunken daisy.

Carry Grant called me - in the early afternoon - to talk of Greta Garbo who says she's Jewish, but, Grant says she isn't. She's too busy starving herself, he says, to be Jewish. He was pro-Godard and Idris Elba. Garbo, in contrast, was whimsical, cruel, and exploitative, too! You experienced her ferity - immediately - after your first encounter at a water fountain. She's traded in her fox furs for light-weight, wrinkle free, button down shirts.

After dinner, we watched more *Manifest*. We are at the scene in which Ben, less buff and less muscular, bribed his way into seeing the wingtail of the Montego 828 from two lucrative, thrill seeking fishmen. Cal looked round - and cute - and Zeke looked fit and handsome. By the end of the first episode of the third season,

your lips were feverishly laminating your skin. Your gaze was one of hunger and manic curiosity. I felt the intermittent pyretic kisses that your lips left trailing on my exposed neck. Our lovemaking was rich in oak. We were crustacean, marine-like and elongated. When I sprawled out on our minimal bed with slanted cedar-colored round slats, you looked at me as if I was everything you wanted that evening: endless euphoria bursting forth like champagne. Even if the night soaked its inebriated soul in ash, you had the gaze of great love for me.

Now weekends don't seem so old or gray. Before we fall asleep, you tell me I have the type of intelligence that walks away from itself. Yesterday afternoon I walked myself into my own *Bewilderment*. I thought *Manifest* is a cosmic joke and I remembered laughing alone at a drugstore in April. While filling a prescription for lexapro, I sobbed and laughed out loud because it was the kind of joke my brother loved. Back then I laughed a lot. I thought it was a cosmic joke, life, what I know, and I thought *he is with me* and I thought *we are laughing*. The heat moved over the car and the asphalt like a mirage. We called my brother "bird."

One night in April, my balcony trapped a hummingbird. It fluttered, frantically, at the sliding door, its beak tapping the glass and, naturally, I thought my brother was the bird. He loved *Slouching Toward Bethlehem* best. From Louisiana to Arkansas, I listened. On the way to his funeral, there was a sign for Jamestown and a sign for Williamsburg. I laughed. I said *Jesus Christ.* I said *I get it.* I drove into a hailstorm. A fourteen wheeler nearly blew my car over. I whispered *be with me.* I sobbed into the steering wheel. Or was it rain? It rained so much like Van Gogh smeared my windshield with the madness of a landscape. I thought, No one wants to leave. You disagreed. *Jess,* you texted me, *good morning. How did you sleep?* A giant truck blew past, flung a puddle of rainwater at my eyes and I winced at an impact I did not, in fact, experience.

The next morning, you sent me a text. You said: *Good morning Jess. How did you sleep?* I slept well. That summer I fell in love with you and driving. I sat still and was in motion. The truth is, I watched for something to take shape in the darkness. Maybe, I was awaiting your intelligence, which is patient and fatalistic. Like you laid down in mystery

and never got up again. *Jess,
I have a question,* you said.
*Jess, would you marry a man
you hated for a hundred years, if
it meant, eventually, you'd be
united with the love of your life?*
Yes, I said, I guess I'd do it. One
of these days, you told
me, we'll invest in a meat
cutter.

YOUR GEOMETRY IS SO APPARENT

On the other side of the blue asphalt, stray cats yowl at garbage drums. My father signed me up for the Army in a dream last night. His smile was intact and profoundly white.

Tomorrow we will wake again. You, in the early morning before the sun has risen. You zip your trim torso into a coat and raise the collar against the cold. The grass is slick with sleep and you wait in it for the Uber. The dexterity and certainty of your hands holding an avocado. Take your time. There is more of it.

There will always be more of it until there isn't. You showed me your wrist in another Zoom video, and you had time even in your forced criminalization today to count how many times you peed. Did you lose 10 pounds of water weight in one day? Is your heart being inefficient again?

I ran today to avoid my time with meatballs and to invite a more intimate relationship with brussel sprouts. They are these vegetable mammals

that are micro-planets in themselves. Each time I bite into one I think of other gas giants. The kind that won't visit my father in his dreams of me. I would join the army for him if he would tell me why I am his favorite child and why he bought that extravagant ring for my mother twenty five years ago. I want to know what kind of an apology can exist only as a heavy circle. Months later, in front of an old digital dictionary, I learned that there is an anus in annulus. Somewhere under all the screenshots you were speaking.

You were lost in the documentation of our changing faces. You showed me a photograph of you in a yellow dress. Your hair was almost amber. The sun shone through the cracks in a splintered barn wall. And I wondered who took it and was there another one of you rushing through trees whose inflorescent descent captured the engine of life rowing its boat. Its oars were wooden and muscular like your back when you crawled across the white desert years ago for a lover whose love bifurcated in a bathtub.

You think of this in a straight back chair gazing out your office window. The sky is blue as gas fire and the clouds really do look like cotton balls in a ziplock bag. You are the image of self-possession. The angle of your hand holding your chin, and the angle of your collar bisecting your mouth. You watch a cloud yawn into a mountain. Come back. Last year you sat with a collection of bright round ornaments in the background, and read of an old lover whose love you felt only when she told you to leave her. Because only one who looks so perfectly complete and solitary can know such things. Your fatalistic pose, your eyes static as an expiration date, or a sealed balloon that bursts against a brick building. I kept on staring at your sleeves for clarity of desire. I underestimated how famished I could be in seeing your fingers fluttering on screen, becoming soft fog with its algebra masking its inferior axiom. Because how could I not want to kiss you or hold you when your geometry is so apparent.

I am bent over, reading my notes from years ago. In the morning I taught two classes whose faces became the mirror of my pedagogy. My students did show up - sharing the screen or the embroidery of their quotidian lives. They are young and unevenly shy. Even Zoomed out, I am entitled to keep wanting you. I am entitled to your soft lips. My pale, etiolated exposed neck - all yours - hemp and rice straw-ready for you as if I am a potato plant that has been soaked in coconut water overnight. When I ran again later tonight, each foot I laid down was starchy like tapioca flour. Each step I took was cellophane - only diaphanous after my sweat disappeared from view. I buried old terms of pith, cut thin into ice, only suitable for liminal moments.

At the grocery store, I caressed a pear, then an avocado, then the vulnerable, lush head of the cabbage and thought of you. Of your exposed clavicle while you were shaking the strainer with the noodle in it and how much I wanted to devour you, run my tongue through your defenseless banana-shaped earlobe, and pull you into me.

In another classroom, your students, listless then attuned as rabbits, trembled when you stood beside them. It's ok, you said, to tremble. Your diaphanous pink dress was thin enough for me to feel the heat of your skin if I put my hand against it. You are ill in all your author photos and this afternoon you sent me those taken before the surgeons opened you. Your angular fingers folded around two pomegranates, their shadows small and flat against your breast. And the shadows of your fingers like spider's legs on a hardwood floor, the green vines falling on your neck. And the rug? The rug was shaggy and white like your winter coat.

In the morning, my brother visited my dream. He fired a pink rifle into the sky.

He'd dine with a fork and knife while driving. In a snowstorm, on a narrow mountain road, he programmed his phone to call his lesbian sister on command. I said, watch the road. He asked whether I thought that he would kill us. He promised not to kill us, and then he almost did. He hit a deer instead. He called it "lightly tapped." The deer fell down. Then skittered to its feet and leapt between two trees. Later, standing in the dry cold outside the car, we noticed a tuft of tail fur stuck behind the headlight.

I told you all of this in the early Friday morning when the crickets had not been experiencing insomnia. And, you wrote, "Anger - the beginning of acceptance." It seems unavoidable that I am moving through the steps slowly. I am like a hairpin traveling through and down a tall silo filled with blooming chia seeds. Yet, the morning seems to have gotten to know my body too well.

And, even my dreams too which cake everything that appears slippery and gray like a fish beating its head and tail against a plank of wood. Sometimes I'd feel like Didion, whipping her car around some California mountain. In the summer heat, I started running. In the wind and breeze, I'd touch my eyes and discover I'd been crying.

Mid-morning, mid-orgasm, it happened again. You clasped me with your arms and legs, and I sobbed into your neck and you sang me the strangest song I'd ever heard and I could not understand the words though my breathing slowed

　　　　and 　　　my 　　　grief
folded 　　　like 　　　an
umbrella into your
chest.

I am aware, too, In the early
afternoon, that you are on an Uber
ride to your next Airbnb. Colorado
sprawls, high altitude desert.
Someone sends a video of my brother
eating at a restaurant in Delhi. The fan
spins on my ceiling. It is the dull grey
dawn of a Louisiana storm and
lightning snaps the sky's waistband.

TAKE O UT YOUR PHONE & GOOGLE IT!

The temperature drops to 50 at night and after sunrise heat climbs the day's spine to 80. The early mornings are crisp & so cold. At the station, the sky spread her post-apocalyptic wings, striations of hueish pink and blueish gray like the garment of a monarch butterfly,

a man followed me into the elevator.

The PL button lit up no matter what button we pushed, & the elevator did not budge. I climbed several stairs & he climbed beside me, slowly. He looked thin and athletic, he said, "You smell wonderful. What

are you wearing?"
My voice dropped off. I
said I just showered.
He kept pace
with my
slowness. When we
made it to the far side
of the platform, I did
not climb inside the
elevator with him. I
took the stairs down.
"Have a great
day," I said &
hoped I'd never
see him again.

But he
found me waiting for
the train to Union Station.
He zipped his
hoodie over his
head. He looked like a
black and white
Spiderman. "You
wouldn't believe
how much my shoes
cost," he said. "Take
out your phone and
Google it." Since he
kept insisting that I
Google it and since he and
I were the only ones on the
platform, I did. I took
out my phone and I
Googled it. I typed in
red, white, and blue and
Adidas and NERD and I
discovered that his

patriotic tennis shoes cost just under 6K. I didn't say anything. I took out my facemask & put it on.

I once thought being in love would close my erotic doors to the world and no one would try to enter. How wrong was my perception?

I tried to find a door which would allow me to dismiss his existence quickly but - the train came & he waited until I got on and then followed. I needed to manspread my small self and so I sat down & placed my bag on the seat beside mine. When the train arrived, I abandoned his existence and I descended the escalator to the Ff1 gate. I took a moment to recover my breath. Policemen were making their daily

morning
rounds, waking up
everyone who slept
on the floor or
sideways inside the un-
accommodating station's
lung. My heart jolted
each time they stirred
someone awake and I
wished they'd just let
the homeless men
sleep.

YOUR DRESS IS A SWEATING DAFFODIL

Outside, the air is heavy as droplets of coruscating water swimming through a bowl of eggnog. Suddenly the sound of something from the interior periphery pulls me back in.

Is it the sound of the microwave beeping or is it you telling me how you seductively requested my address a day or two ago that leaves me feeling like I am submerged in linen?

Even though landmines are not children of Covid, you are quick to tell me that the heavy smoke from the fire is only smoke and could equally be the other side of something,
a country where the yellow light falls on broad green leaves and the walkways are made of weeping concrete.

Your yellow dress is like a sweating daffodil, the dampness on your brow, where strands of hair get stuck. If you were the bathhouse and I was the linen we could both be the eloquent things that kitchen sinks are made of: floating water, restless foam, disembodied utensils. Our home is silent. And, sits like an old woman chewing betel nuts while gazing far near a Panda Chrome poet and whispering, "When you are no longer driftwood soaked in poseidon blood, I want to make love to you near a papaya tree." And, I think your left cheek is chalky like you rubbed your face in the foam around the mountain's jowls and now you've come back down and I wonder was I with you?

Meanwhile, the sky asks for its vapor back and your eyes, with your head against a pillowless bed, are gazing past me at A spot looming on the ceiling. And I wonder whether you're in love with San Francisco's canola bars? Are you pregnant with powdered strawberries? Will you kiss my left eyelid before you brush the coconut
water off your book's spine? Or tell your tongue that it has ached my avocado-smittened saliva all morning?

When I wake, your breath is a million light years away. The light falls on where you often fall in the seven days that made up the religion of collarbones flanked by a forest of trees or wrists deep in soapy dish water.

With you embedded in my arms, the persimmon tree at our nearby Airbnb seems less lonely and less forlorn. Its fruits so verdant, the kind of green that made you think of the colors a CEO would finalize for sleeping bags. Our bodies are trying not to be Styrofoam with one another, leaning without buoyancy and without being able to decompose each other in the feverish embrace. I have been torn not like a page out of a book while you pressed your face deeper into my neck. But, I am torn, my agony resides in the policy--

The connection clears its throat, drowns your voice in static, and a distant siren threads the silence. Your lips move but your mouth is soundless. My mind finishes a sentence yours began. This time my chest tightens and I wait for you. I want to understand how you are torn. I flip through your book, listless & waiting for you, but the page I want is gone: a bumble bee crowning a glorious nest of wheat, your hands hanging limp between your knees, the damp hair on your temple like splintered twigs or a teacup's tiny fracture.

If I could turn my armpits into mittens, I'd slip your hands in them, because your hands are strong and delicate and break nothing but themselves and sit like queens at the ends of your wrists. I'd make my arms into thrones and my armpits into red and gold flesh cushions. Or how my cunt waits like a china hutch, where the plates are wide and long and decorated with wet paint pigments crushed morosely by a watercolor dancer and a few cucumbers. The night is soft like a quiet breakfast without a sweater over it or an engine with its tongue tucked inside its skirt. I kiss you lavishly, one cheekbone at a time. Our kitchen door opens widely. Its bruised lips are red with rubyish radiance. There is clarity in its creaking.

It's whispering *remember when…*in another city you grew faint and fell down. I grazed the back of your hand. In Louisiana, you held my cracked umbrella and your hands
were sure though you are not the sort to keep a door when the hinges break, or if a dish chips to simply let it stay that way.

Even the tips of your fingers stay focused around the rim of your teacup with a wedge of lemon and the steam rising up. Your eyes were placid and under my blouse the sun rose and set and dusk fell through the window and over the table and your fork was poised over your plate. So I wring my heart into the basin of our bed and twist my leg around you like a corkscrew rush. In the early morning, before the light meets all the other lights, you'll shake my heart out, and watch the molecules of my desire bite the tongue of your photons. The dense neurons of my caress radiating beneath you, beneath the limelight of these remote charged electrons.

I am positive our love is nuclear energy, invisible only to those who are blind and congenital. I am positive that to touch you, from afar, in my sleep is no criminal enterprise. Even if history blindfolds itself with the anachronistic handkerchief of myth, I still want to press you into the muddy wall and the mulberry bushes. Here the tree's mottled shadows

press their backs against the buildings and hold their breath. There is no breeze, only heat and the sound of a lawnmower's engine advancing and retreating. Midday clouds bow low to the treetops, and the branches twist and ball the shade into their fists. In the evening, your speech is soft and sleepy, like sunken stones and floating driftwood, gathered one by one, and exquisitely arranged in the

faint   and   final   spurts   of   a
menstruating sun.

Or how your barred teeth nailed me
to the mast of last night's sinking
ship, which I had not thought would
sink so quick, and I held
your head between my hands and
down we went. I woke in the red
dawn of another day. Our blue
shadows beneath the lamplight. The
bus panting like a dog, dying,
and whining. A handful of tired men
with rumpled shirts
and dirty backpacks walked past and
I cupped your skull
like a cracked vase and pressed your
heart so hard to mine I
could not tell whose heart beat on my
chest. The
bus coughed black clouds into the
lungs of this, my catatonic
city, then the street cleared its throat
quickly
and left me at the entrance of a vacant
day, waving.

IN THE WEST MY HAIR LOOKS INCREDIBLE

As the great stock broker, Jesse Livermore, once so keenly advised, "Don't be a listless drifter." And, yet, it was inevitable: you were drifting. Listlessly, even. Losing cash as you went, plummeting our relationship into an intermittent act of evacuation.

I fluttered between Houston and Shreveport and Dallas. All the hotels and Airbnbs were booked out. A line of pickups wound around gas pumps and into the interstate. Maskless men in mesh hats pumped gallons of gas into red cans and toilet paper stuck to all the bathroom floors.

Later, I'll laugh at all the
Subarus at the Trader Joe's.
I'll marvel at how slow the cars
go, how the trucks do not
trample the hem of my
dress, or how the freshly
paved roads have no
potholes.
How crisp the morning air;
I'll wake cold with you
clasped to me. I'll block a
bike path with my stopped
car, and a gray and grizzly
haired cyclist in a puffy
vest and bike helmet will
practically snap his neck to
puncture our bovine delight
with his withering eyes
and our Boulder bliss will
wheeze out of us. We'll turn to
each other and agree: but the
people, they are assholes,
aren't they?

Here the brown bike paths
wind under mountains
and spit cyclists out like
fireballs, or ghosts in pac-man,
they materialize at each
intersection, shaking their heads
and waving their fingers,
before vanishing under a canopy
of lush lush trees.

All that awaited me at the end of an endless day. And so, I did not think of Colorado while I pumped gas in the hazy Louisiana heat. I was preparing myself for the safe and lonely life that I believed awaited me. A manageable and small life organized by to do lists, a life, I had convinced myself that remained manageable only through constant vigilance. I felt physically sick. And, then the hurricane in my body left and with it, the lightening body striated itself across the infinite, desolate horizon of Texas.

There were tumbleweeds curling themselves into curling irons that matched the landscape as we passed one desolate horizon to the next. As we drifted there were less and less people on the road. We even stopped by the Big Texan for steak and fries. I observed these elegant women who excelled in the art of self-care with their hands on these beer belly drinking men. They looked as greasy as the things they ate. While waiting for our 8 oz steak, I overheard a man telling his girlfriend how gay his dog is. "He is just so gay!" And this accented homophobia also married itself to a scene earlier: a mannequin in an electric chair donned in a black and white striped prison uniform being electrocuted in a death penalty style. I wanted to take you away from all of this wrong endorphin. I did not want you to use the bathroom or wait under the covered porch while I pulled the car around. The ugly man with the gay dog said New Orleans was flushing its toilet. Meanwhile Ida drifted listlessly east.

Seats inside the Big Texan were shaped like saddles. For four quarters, you could shoot up some dummies in western suits. I asked whether you'd like to and you said you would not. There was a wooden

shed with a sign on the door that said "one dollar for a good time." I was afraid of everyone. Outside the clouds grew thick and grey. It seemed somehow like something from a horror movie or something built too many decades ago to still be so popular.

All that awaited me at the end of an endless day. And so, I did not think of Colorado while I pumped gas in the hazy Louisiana heat. I was preparing myself for the safe and lonely life that I believed awaited me on the other side of a hurricane.

Far Wall told you not to stand in the way of your own happiness. She said, my love is rare and special. I asked *whether you believe that's true.* You told me you did not know. And all the way to Dallas, I'd wondered whether all your other loves were just like this. Did you leave them easily; the way you almost left me? *It is,* I said, *special, Vi.* I don't say I could see myself settling down with you, as though this were a concession with monumental dimensions. I don't mark off what I do and do not like about you. I never planned it; to take you only in a red dress. To love you polished. You drift off and forget the sentence that you started and I look over at you while driving and you say, "Why are you smiling?" We barely made it out of death penalty Texas when I professed what I already knew best: our love is impractical because it has red wine, chocolate, and an avocado smoothie in it.

In the morning, while I drove us both to Boulder campus where the jaywalking and carefree and careless bikers leapt and jumped in and out of my periphery, I felt overwhelmed. Like I could run over anyone at any given moment. Every parking lot seemed to require a permit even though we had to pay sort of an arm and a leg for it. In your office, you tell me how white Boulder is. There isn't even a single black student in both sections of your class. Before falling asleep, you looked so sad. When we turned off the air conditioner, I tossed and turned all night. I was overheated or too hot. Your chair called you into his office to tell you the students could not understand your speech. In your bed you wondered how I could feel close to you. Was it because my white world had rejected me?

We felt like guests in the kitchen that evening. Had to remind ourselves we paid for this. Interlopers to a party we were declined an invitation. We floated over it like helium trapped inside a balloon, whose flotation was not in celebration of a stranger, but your breathless smile, the radiance of being inside each other's company again. And the others bobbed us up and down. It did not matter. You stirred the meat, the scent of our cooking filled the kitchen. We ate like siblings from a single bowl.

When we turned off the air conditioner, I tossed and turned all night. I was overheated or too hot.

The mountains look purple in the morning. Your mouth is like cold water. I teach my storm drenched class about Frederick Douglass and outside the UC Boulder students dance in the Colorado sunshine. Soon you will return to me lighter than when you left, I think, and then you're back, wearing your black jumpsuit with white polka-dots. You prop your legs on the tabletop and floss. My lecture notes were sprawled out on my desk like a soccer team - each line, each player drifting to a field of words.

Teaching on Zoom is something else entirely. It could be demoralizing talking to blank screens. Screens belonging to my students whose homes and lives have been submerged under water. Hurricane Ida continued to visit relatives up north - where New York and New England reside. My phone continued to explode - my colleagues in Louisiana tell me about the hurricane. From time to time, I gazed back at you - sitting in a sinking chair in your office. When class ended, I crawled into your arms and tried to sleep my deep deprivation away. My exhaustion - its inevitability is a door I could easily slip through. Yesterday, I had accused you of being callous.

When the Amazon packages arrived - dried mangos, black foamy facemasks, creamy onion chips - you bestowed on me the impression that you'd keep the gifts but toss my notes away. I suppose I can be a fool, easily disappointed. You would be going to a reading tonight. A reading I could not attend. I pulled from my wallet a five dollar bill: the entry fee for attending Stephen Graham Jones' reading and gave it to you. You gazed at it as if you didn't understand what money was. Later, I learned that my thoughtful gesture appeared infinitely wife-like to you - like it doesn't matter if my hair looks incredible or not. I had him as an instructor a

long time ago, when I was in Utah. He brought everyone Chick-fil-A and was kind. It is easy to tell you that you would like him. He is not white and I get the sense that you would not feel alone in Boulder's morbid whiteness. I get the sense that I can only help you halfway with that loneliness. In the evening, I listened to men talk to one another about their work and their wives, and sat, listlessly, like a patient child. It is so humiliating to be among men, to be the only woman, or to be among women whose instinct is to protect those men from ever knowing their offenses.

Last night, I dreamt that I moved my ticketed car while a student waited in my office. In the midst of my fanatic rush, I realized I could kill someone driving like that, and tried to slow down, but realized that I could no longer remember whether the break was the big or small pedal. Meanwhile, you needed an aunt to reveal the truth about your ancestry. You broke into a pharmacy, and stole a truth serum. The night before, I dreamt that I'd returned to high school after the summer of my brother's death and I no longer knew how to be a student. An old friend from high school, Alex Leon, noticed this and tried, in hushed tones, to show me, but we looked around & knew that we were being watched. I thought she is so kind, to risk so much. I did not want to push her kindness. I was certain that I was hopeless. So I feigned comprehension. These dreams arrived to me as if begging me to change the clothes of my trepidation and anxiety. I had slept naked the night before with you. The pill I took slipped down my throat without a fight.

The air from the mountain has descended bringing elongated ski boots with it and converted our pre-soporific nights into chilly mornings. I mourned my mornings whenever we couldn't sleep in. I know we must exit our Airbnb. Our host treated us like guests instead of tenants and so there were no boundaries between what we could do and what belonged to us. When our space met her space, she had a way of making us feel like intruders. We even packed the night before. Our shoes, mine and yours, traveled inconspicuously on our

Subaru floor. When our lips met in the early Boulder hour, you recalled none of your dreams. Though Far Wall was in a terrible mood because she slept so poorly. I put my hair up and drank coffee. You gazed at me lovingly while you baked literary pies with Sarah. You kept telling me how much you loved our love making last night.

You called it meditative and unassuming. By mid-morning, we left our Airbnb. The whole place smelled like dog pee and I thought the chihuahua's penis was way too big. Finding parking on lot 282 was impossible for us. It was booked all out several nights ago.

Perhaps there is pertinent drinking culture here - where folks wanted to drink the nights away without having to roam the mountains for decent or nonexistent parking. The windows in Denver are enormous and the cranes bend their necks over the buildings like antelopes drinking from a stream. I remember the sunlight in Boulder one morning flashed so red between the crowns of trees, I thought a silent siren was wailing. Your face feels soft as the skin of a nectarine. At the grocery in Boulder, no one would help the woman in the wheelchair. In Boulder the cars behave as if their lane is property they paid for, and their drivers blow their horns or glare when you enter them. In late afternoon, the students moved in large groups, holding red plastic cups, which seemed somehow alien to the brown and green landscape, like a tv in the desert with no one to watch. You seemed frenzied that morning in the office, and in the afternoon, Jeffrey walked you back to Hellem.

The air from the mountain has descended bringing elongated ski boots with it and converted our pre-soporific nights into chilly mornings.

It really isn't a driver friendly city, I was thinking, that evening when I saw you standing outside the bookstore and the crowds were like foam spilling out of a dishwasher and flooding the street. The light turned red and I shouted from my car window. It is so nice to build a life with someone. It is a pleasure I have never known. At the airbnb, you asked about our lovemaking. What has changed? You said I was so tender. And I did not know how to answer, save that I missed you, and there is so much pleasure in this, holding each other inside our daily existence. There was pleasure and distraction. Your eyes rolled off the side of my face. I stood in a towel. You were telling me something, but your sentence drifted. There were moments when we seemed to be holding parallel conversations,

like two roads running
alongside one another. It was
like trying to make a left turn in
Boulder, and some grassy, well-
kept division between the lanes
kept us from each other's
minds.

It really isn't a driver friendly
city, I was thinking, that
evening when I
saw you standing outside the
bookstore and the crowds were
like   foam
             spilling out of a
dishwasher The light

                              tu
rned   red   and   I
shouted   from
my car window.
Your eyes rolled off the side
of my face.

I stood
in   a

towel.

It is so nice to build a life with someone. It is a pleasure I have never known. At the airbnb, you asked about our lovemaking. What has changed? You said I was so tender. And I did not know how to answer, save that I missed you, and there is so much pleasure in this, holding each other inside our daily existence. There was pleasure and distraction. Your eyes rolled off the side of my face. I stood in a towel. You were telling me something, but your sentence drifted. There were moments when we seemed to be holding parallel conversations, like two roads running alongside one another. It was like trying to make a left turn in Boulder, and some grassy, well-kept division between the lanes keeps us.

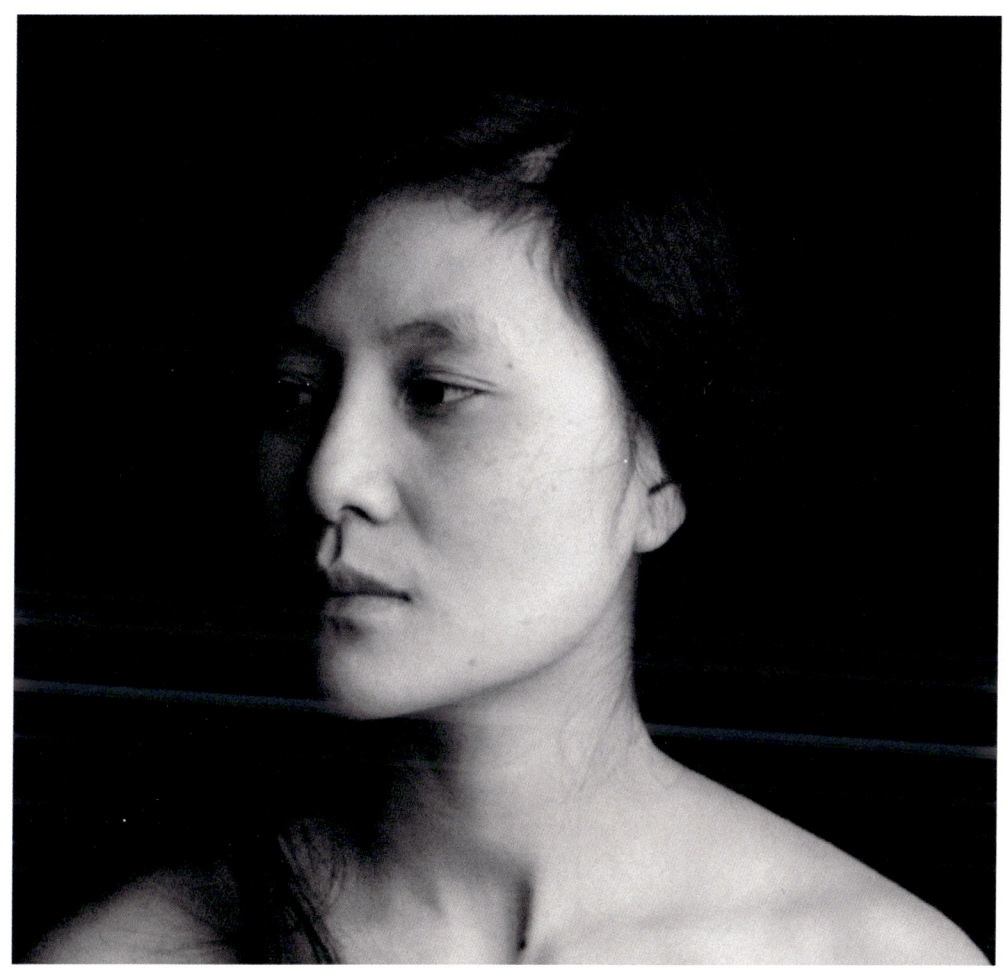

VI KHI NAO earned her B.A. in Art & Spanish from Central College and an M.F.A from Brown University. She is the author of five poetry collections: *A Bell Curve Is A Pregnant Straight Line* (Press 11:11, 2021), *Human Tetris* (11:11 Press, 2019) *Sheep Machine* (Black Sun Lit, 2018), Umbilical Hospital (Press 1913, 2017), *The Old Philosopher* (winner of the Nightboat Prize for 2014), & of the short stories collection, *A Brief Alphabet of Torture* (winner of the 2016 FC2's Ronald Sukenick Innovative Fiction Prize), the novel, *Fish in Exile* (Coffee House Press, 2016). She is an interdisciplinary artist who works in multiple and interchangeable mediums. Her drawings have appeared in literary journals such as *NOON* and *The Adirondack Review* . Her video, digital, and literary installations have been exhibited at the Perry and Marty Granoff Center for the Creative Arts in Providence in Rhode Island and in the largest exhibition halls for contemporary art in Europe, Malmö Konsthall, in Sweden. Her work includes poetry, fiction, nonfiction, performance, film and cross-genre collaboration. She was the Fall 2019 fellow at the Black Mountain Institute. https://www.vikhinao.com

JESSICA ALEXANDER earned an MA at Ohio University and her PhD at the University of Utah. Alexander's work explores trauma and the power of violent comedy through the parodic repetition of old forms. She has given talks and taught courses on queering the thriller, the poetics of queer comedy, and hauntology. Her story collection, *Dear Enemy* explores the barbed though familiar form of fairytales, coupling their fatalistic simplicity—the paratactic, transition-less shift from small talk to death—with a blithe, whimsical, and often ecstatic narrative voice. *Dear Enemy*, was the winning manuscript in the 2016 Subito Prose Contest, as judged by Selah Saterstrom. Her novella, "None of This Is an Invitation" (co-written with Katie Jean Shinkle) is forthcoming from Astrophil Press in the spring of 2023. Her fiction has been published in journals such as *Fence, Black Warrior Review, PANK, Denver Quarterly, The Collagist, and DIAGRAM*. She lives in Louisiana where she serves as Co-Director of the Creative Writing Program and teaches Fiction at the University of Louisiana at Lafayette. https://www.jessica-alexander.com